The

HEART *of*
HOLINESS

The

HEART *of* HOLINESS

Compassion and the Holy Life

CARL M. LETH, EDITOR

Nazarene Publishing House
Kansas City, Missouri

Copyright © 2015 by Nazarene Publishing House
Nazarene Publishing House
PO Box 419527
Kansas City, MO 64141
NPH.com

ISBN 978-0-8341-3518-5

Printed in the
United States of America

Cover Design: Mike Williams
Interior Design: Sharon Page

The Internet addresses, email addresses, and phone numbers in this book
are accurate at the time of publication. They are provided as a resource. Nazarene Publishing House does not endorse them or vouch for their content
or permanence.

10 9 8 7 6 5 4 3 2 1

CONTENTS

PREFACE

● ●

This book is the culmination of a process that began in a series of individual conversations. Those conversations resulted in a formal roundtable event involving a representative range of participants from across the country. They gathered for two days, hosted by Jay Height at Shepherd Community in Indianapolis in early 2013. One of the outcomes of that meeting was the decision to pursue this conversation further in a public forum at Olivet Nazarene University. Olivet's Ella M. Fruin Holiness Endowment for the Fruin Holiness Series provided both opportunity and funding for this forum. In February 2014 the conference gathered resource people from across the country with pastors from the Olivet regions and students from Olivet for a two-day conversation on the place of compassion in the holy life. The contributions in this book were drawn from that conference and developed for this further discussion.

INTRODUCTION
WELCOME TO THE CONVERSATION
Carl M. Leth

● ●

A Place to Begin

Compassion is a Jesus quality. Seeing need, Jesus' natural reaction was to be moved with compassion (Matt. 9:35-38; Mark 6:34). He was moved—and moved to act (Matt. 14:14). Of course, this was no new revelation of God's character. The exodus of the people of Israel, arguably the defining event in their history, is prompted by God's compassion for them (Exod. 2:23-25). The incarnation itself is God's movement of compassion. "For God so loved the world that he gave his one and only Son" (John 3:16). This conversation about compassion concerns a core characteristic of God's life. To live in the likeness of Christ means being moved with compassion.

The question, then, is not whether compassion is important, even essential, but how we should understand and practice it. What is the place of compassion in the holy life? This is the question we are considering in this book. As a holy (holiness) people, how should we understand and practice compassion—both personally and in the ministry of the church?

9

This is, of course, not a new conversation. Our relatively recent history as a tradition has included reanimated conversation around this question. In the early 1970s, as a young seminary student, the place of compassion in our tradition was revisited by leaders such as Tom Nees. New, highly visible ministries such as The Lamb's Club in New York and the Community of Hope in Washington, D.C., posed new possibilities. The conversation expanded and ministries of compassion began to emerge across the country. Those ministries began to be recognized and affirmed by denominational leaders. Compassionate ministry moved into the life of the American church.

A Continuing Conversation

This book is an effort to continue the conversation. It is, however, not a conversation taking place in isolation from other current conversations. We are in a time of significant change, both in our society and in the life and ministry of the church. Our understanding of who we are (at our best), what holiness should look like, and what the missional church should look like are issues of active and vigorous discussion—even debate. Our consideration of compassion needs to take account of these broader conversations. Let me note a few.

Generational changes are posing considerable challenges to how we speak, think, and engage young people who are increasingly affected by postmodernity and the shifting values of that still-uncertain but clearly emerging cultural paradigm. Decreasing patterns of denominational—or confessional—loyalties are being replaced by contextual or occasional partnerships of thought or action. General concerns about compassion and social issues and generalized spiritual interest are largely disconnected from organized religious institutions. The increasing proportion of "nones," who disclaim any religious connection, indicates an increasingly secular perspective among the young. They care about compassion but fail to see the connection between practices of compassion and organized churches.

We are also witnessing a potential sea change in the shape of congregational ministry in America. An increasingly adversarial culture poses a new ministry context. Heightened financial challenges are calling into question traditional financial models. Bivocational ministry, alternative strategies for church facilities, and creative ministry approaches are present wherever you look. Fundamental missional questions are being posed of traditional ministry models. What does it mean to live and minister as a faithful and effective kingdom community? It is not yet clear what we will be, but it seems clear that future ministry will look different from the church we have inherited. The place of ministries of compassion in the life and practices of the church is an important component of that development.

At the same time, globalization is revealing dynamic growth and effectiveness. The international church is becoming a resource and model from which we can benefit. More holistic models of ministry are producing effectively growing church communities. Ministries of compassion are more generally assumed as normal expressions of congregational ministry. Education, community development, and care for the sick and needy are integrated into church practices without any detriment to more traditional practices of evangelism. For a culture that highly values pragmatism we are witnessing models of ministry that work more effectively than our own.

In fact, our own assumptions about evangelism and discipleship are being examined. The pervasive influences of reformed evangelicalism are being recognized and challenged. The denominational emphasis on producing Christlike disciples counters the more narrow soteriology of reformed evangelicalism. It is not enough to make a "decision." Christ calls us to a changed life. This pronounced transformational emphasis of the holiness tradition is being revisited and reclaimed. The expectation of a radical transformation of heart and life calls us to different ways of living. The quality and practice of compassion must be part of that revisioning.

Discerning a Way Forward

The challenges of living in a time of such significant change also pose significant opportunities. For those who can engage the discomfort and difficulties of these challenges effectively and faithfully, the future becomes a door of opportunity. The valley of troubles can become a "door of hope" (Hos. 2:15). So, how do we do that?

Our faithful attention to the place of compassion in the holy life is an important aspect of that project. As we look for resources and models for the understanding and practice of compassion, it is clear our best options will not involve defaulting to contemporary assumptions and cultural fads. We will be best served by a serious and careful attention to the resources of our inherited tradition. Biblical, historically classic Christian, and Wesleyan-Holiness traditional resources can provide us with rich resources to guide and enrich our understanding and practice. While contemporary insights and models may be helpful to us, it will be the legacy of the Spirit's work among God's people through history that can provide a sound foundation for engaging this uncertain future.

This book is an attempt to do that work.

one

JOURNEY INWARD, JOURNEY OUTWARD
OUR HERITAGE OF COMPASSION

Tom Nees

• •

The organizers of this conversation are to be commended for connecting the themes of holiness and compassion. This emphasis could enhance the holiness message among those within as well as outside the Wesleyan-Holiness tradition.

It could prevent the holiness message, and holiness people, from being eccentric, that is, off-center from historic Christian belief and practice. While John Wesley and Phineas Bresee created new faith communities, they were adamant that they were not introducing some new previously unknown belief or religious experience.

The denominations that emerged from the Holiness Movement of the nineteenth and twentieth centuries understandably emphasized the spread of scriptural holiness or entire sanctification as their reason for existence. The "come outers" who left their traditions to join the new holiness churches were sure they had something to contribute to the larger Christian community. But as time went on the message at times became garbled. Perhaps it was distorted by exaggeration—as Mildred Wynkoop suggested in her *Theology of Love*.[1] As it is with personal strengths, organizational strengths (particularly in faith communities) face a potential pitfall—too much of a good thing.

In the wake of nineteenth-century revivalism, holiness (or entire sanctification) was explained as a conversion-like religious experience following initial salvation. Secondness as a personal experience was seen as an entry point into the life of holiness, de-emphasizing if not opposing Wesley's more contemplative faith journey. Holiness or entire sanctification as a private individual experience became defined, and to some extent still is, as adherence to rules of conduct often tending toward legalisms. And since holiness was often identified with perfectionism, believers who could not measure up were never quite sure whether or not they were sanctified.

The life and practice of holiness was further distorted by abandoning, if not opposing the social reform commitments of the early Holiness Movement in place from the time of Wesley until the early twentieth century. Absent this engagement with the quality of life issues around them, holiness people seemed more interested in preserving their tradition than changing the world. For those influenced by early twentieth-century premillennialism and fundamentalism, belief in the experience of holiness was more important than practice: orthodoxy vs. orthopraxis. Uprooted from its origins, the Holiness Movement seemed increasingly isolated and eccentrically overemphasizing one important biblical theme.

By intentionally bringing holiness and compassion together, this conference has an opportunity to lead the Holiness Movement forward, centered in historic Christianity. By renewing the practice (praxis) of holiness with its inward and outward dimensions, the message will prove relevant for a new generation of believers who want to change the world for the better as their own lives have been changed.

The phrase "journey inward, journey outward" describes my own experience within the Wesleyan-Holiness tradition. Soon after graduating from Nazarene Theological Seminary in 1962, I served as pastor of the Church of the Nazarene in Sunnyvale, California, near the epicenter of the sixties social protests, the antiwar hippies in San Francisco's Haight-Ashbury neighborhood, and the Free Speech Movement erupting on the Berkeley campus of the University of California.

I remember well when President Kennedy was assassinated in 1963, and then Martin Luther King Jr. on April 4, 1968, and soon after on June 6, Robert Kennedy. Add to that the advancing civil rights movement. I was troubled during this tumultuous era—as was Thomas Merton in his meditations, *Conjectures of a Guilty Bystander*[2]—because my tradition frowned on social engagement.

During that time, I was challenged by Elizabeth O'Connor's *Call to Commitment*,[3] the story of the ecumenical Church of the Saviour founded by Gordon Cosby[4] in Washington, D.C., in 1946, upon his return from duty as an Army chaplain in World War II.

It was a church with Jesuit-like membership requirements of spiritual exercises combined with engagement with the social problems of the city. I thought then that if I ever got to Washington, D.C., I wanted to see it firsthand. I could not have imagined as I watched Washington, D.C., neighborhoods engulfed in flames following the assassination of Martin Luther King Jr. that I would soon begin a twenty-five-year ministry in one of those so-called riot corridors.

By the time I began my ministry at the Washington, D.C., First Church of the Nazarene in 1971, O'Connor had published another book, *Journey Inward, Journey Outward*,[5] the story of how the Church of the Saviour reinvented itself around mission groups with members accountable to spiritual directors for disciplines of prayer, Scripture reading, journaling, and silence, while engaging in neighborhood service projects.

I joined a mission group soon after my arrival that included Pastor Gordon Cosby. Our initial mission was to wait tables each Thursday evening at the Potter's House. During that time we were becoming more aware of the low-income housing crisis close by. In response, we organized Jubilee Housing to acquire deteriorating apartment buildings and help the low-income residents rehab and eventually own their own buildings.

During the early seventies, with a few members of First Church, I agreed to organize our own mission group and take responsibility for a forty-eight-unit deteriorating building in the so-called riot corridor of northwest Washington, D.C., full of people struggling to pay rent. That mission group became the nucleus of the Community of Hope, a ministry that integrated the personal and social dimensions of the gospel, if not holiness.[6] I began to think of the Wesleyan-Holiness narrative as, in the words of O'Connor's book, a journey inward, journey outward.

At the same time I completed a doctor of ministry program at Wesley Theological Seminary (WTS) in Washington, D.C., I had a growing interest in my own tradition, particularly the eighteenth-century evangelical revival in England led by John and Charles Wesley and the formative period of the Church of the Nazarene from the turn of the twentieth century to 1925.

What I found changed my ministry, if not my life. As the assassination of Martin Luther King Jr. was an Isaiah 6 awakening, my discovery of John Wesley and the founders of the Church of the Nazarene was a Josiah (2 Kings 22) experience, discovering within my own tradition the theological and practical foundation and motivation I needed to pursue my calling.

In the Wesleyana section of the WTS library I discovered records of Wesley's engagement with the poor and his voluntary practice of poverty. All I knew from my theology classes in college and prior seminary work were his sermons on holiness, without reference to context. It was never mentioned that the book Wesley wrote and published more than any book of sermons or theology was a book on health care for those for whom medical attention was an unaffordable luxury. That aspect of Wesley was never discussed.

Encouraged from what I was learning about the Wesleyan-Holiness story, I eventually wrote my DMin thesis in 1975: "The Holiness Social Ethic and Nazarene Urban Ministry,"[7] referenced in *Apostles of Reason: The Crisis of Authority in American Evangelicalism*[8] (published by Oxford University Press in 2014) by Molly Worthen, assistant professor of history at the University of North Carolina at Chapel Hill.

The committee reviewing my thesis wanted me to demonstrate that Wesleyan-Holiness theology, as articulated by Wesley and later advanced by the founders of the Church of the Nazarene, is inextricably intertwined with social transformation. It was not enough that these leaders were engaged in serving the poor and advocating for social reforms. The committee wanted me to make the case that holiness theology and practice, necessarily, not just coincidentally, advances social as well as personal transformation.

It seemed clear that the link that connects holiness and compassion is Wesley's emphasis on "perfect love." As Albert Outler, in his volume *John Wesley* from A Library of Protestant Thought puts it:

"Perfect love," as Wesley understood it, is the conscious certainty, *in a present moment*, of the fullness of one's love for God and neighbor, as this love has been initiated and fulfilled by God's gifts of faith, hope and love. This is not a state but a dynamic process: saving faith is its beginning; sanctification is its proper climax. As faith is in order to love, so love is in order to goodness.[9]

This understanding of love, lived out in the second commandment as love of neighbor, was the foundation for Wesley's eventual engagement to improve the dire social conditions of workers during the Industrial Revolution of his day.

Though ordained in the Church of England, Wesley was never assigned to a parish, thus he would say "the world is my parish." Influenced by the open-air evangelist George Whitefield he set aside his high-church instincts and took his message to the fields and streets. Converts from among the working poor, people who were unlikely to be found in the Church of England, responded enthusiastically. This historical context had much to do with how Wesley's social concerns evolved in England and later in America. With its central theme of holiness motivated by "perfect love" of God and neighbor in the midst of poverty and need, the personal and social dimensions of the gospel were integrated within Methodism and the holiness churches that followed.

As my own life and ministry were evolving in the poverty-stricken neighborhood of Washington, D.C., I studied the social reforms advanced by Wesley, the nineteenth-century American Holiness Movement, and the founders of the Church of the Nazarene. In the mid-seventies I spent several weeks in the Nazarene Archives documenting references to social concern and action during the formative period of the Church of the Nazarene from 1895 to around 1925.

In 1970 Mildred Bangs Wynkoop, theology professor at Trevecca Nazarene College (now University), published a series of chapel lectures as *John Wesley: Christian Revolutionary*,[10] followed by her major work, *A Theology of Love*, in 1972. In her lectures she identified "some contemporary Wesleyanisms" that had strayed from Wesley's life and teachings.

Wesley's doctrine, moreover, would not permit him to rest content in biblical theology as such, or religious experience as such—two stopping places for some contemporary Wesleyanisms. Instead it pushed him into the social and economic and educational problems in the world outside his church.

Wesley was one of the first advocates of popular education. He saw that his converts must be cared for, and he built schools wherever enough converts warranted it.

He knew the value of wealth if properly used, but the curse of it when it was controlled by selfish hands. He practiced what he preached by giving away (we are told) 98 percent of his income.

Labor problems and child labor came to his attention. He worked for fair wages, fair prices, and honest, healthy employment.

He applied Christian ethics to a corrupt society. His voice against the liquor traffic ("England's master curse") was potent. He was a powerful antislavery spokesman. Wesley's social reforms leaped the Atlantic Ocean and influenced American social morality more than is recognized.

Prior to 1975 it was not widely known among Nazarenes that at its center the Wesleyan-Holiness tradition had always been intentional about social reform. In his 1976 book *Dis-*

covering an Evangelical Heritage,[11] Donald Dayton documented the wide range of reform movements in the nineteenth century advanced by holiness and other evangelical groups. In *Apostles of Reason*, Worthen notes that Timothy Smith's book *Revivalism and Social Reform*[12] "traced the roots of nineteenth-century social progressivism, normally associated with liberal Protestant theology, to earlier evangelical revivals."[13]

However the mid-twentieth century was a time of significant change. Timothy Smith referred to the fifty years between 1925 and 1975 as "the great reversal" when holiness social concern and reform were nearly forgotten. David O. Moberg, professor of sociology and anthropology at Marquette University, used that phrase for the title of his 1972 book *The Great Reversal: Evangelism Versus Social Concern*[14] to describe how Wesleyans, among others, gave up their social concern in reaction to the social gospel. Dayton also described the demise of those reform movements in the mid-twentieth century.

I discovered the same trend in the archives of early Nazarene documents. In the denomination's formative years, Nazarenes were deeply engaged in a variety of gospel missions, orphanages, and rest cottages—providing refuge for young women, victims of white slavery or prostitution, for instance. This has been well documented and preserved in Stan Ingersol's research for *Rescue the Perishing, Care for the Dying: Sources and Documents on Compassionate Ministries in the Nazarene Archives*.[15]

Although Nazarenes knew something of Bresee's mission work in Los Angeles leading to the founding of the Church of the Nazarene in 1895, it seemed to change, almost suddenly. Fewer churches in the United States and Canada were intentionally reaching out to the poor and needy. Fundamentalist opposition to anything resembling the liberal social gospel movement influenced evangelical and holiness churches.

However, by around 1975 the "great reversal" retrenchment was coming to an end. In 1977, within five years of the first edition, Moberg published a revised edition of *The Great Reversal*, changing the subtitle from "Evangelism Versus Social Concern" to "Evangelism and Social Concern."[16] He recognized that in the early seventies holiness and evangelical leaders were, as he wrote, "reversing the great reversal" in practice as well as in theory.

I have lived through much of the great reversal era, a time when some, in the name of holiness, opposed much of what we now do as compassionate ministry. I began my urban, compassionate ministry in Washington, D.C., just as the integration of holiness and social concern was reemerging.

Where are we now?

To some extent the effects of the great reversal remain. Some within the Wesleyan-Holiness movement have yet to align fully with the theology and practice of holiness as an inward/outward life as advocated by the Wesleys, Bresee, and other founders of the Church of the Nazarene.

When at a Methodist Conference Wesley was asked, "What may we reasonably believe to be God's design in raising up the Preachers called Methodist?" his answer was, "To reform the nation, particularly the church, and to spread scriptural holiness over the land."[17] This was more than adding converts to a new denomination. In fact he didn't want to start a new denomination. That happened in America when the Methodists broke with the Church of England during the Revolutionary War era.

Wesley wanted to change the way Christianity was practiced. He said that there is no holiness without social holiness. By "social" he meant that holiness is lived out in communities of mutual accountability and hospitality. Holiness was more than a personal, individual religious experience.

During Wesley's eighteenth-century evangelical revival, Methodist holiness communities of classes and bands welcomed recent converts from among the poor and marginalized for mutual support and accountability as they set out to "reform the nation," challenging the injustices that perpetuated social as well as spiritual impoverishment.

The rapid spread and growth of the movement was the result of this practice of holiness. To some degree this was true within the nineteenth-century American Holiness Movement. Church growth and evangelism (adding converts) resulted from the practice of scriptural holiness understood as a new community (social) of believers practicing the personal and social dimensions of the gospel.

In 2005 I set out on a project to learn what a few leading preachers in the Church of the Nazarene were preaching about holiness. I was as much interested in what people in the pews were hearing and embracing as in what the scholars were writing. Several preachers sent recorded sermons to transcribe and agreed to interviews. I wanted to know how the message of holiness was being received and how their own understanding of holiness had evolved.

The book was compiled and edited as *Dirty Hands—Pure Hearts: Sermons and Conversations with Holiness Preachers*[18]— from the title of Dan Boone's sermon. I asked Dr. Boone, now president of Trevecca Nazarene University, "How would the people in your congregation describe holiness in their own lives?" He responded,

> I think they would describe it as holy love—the willingness to love the unlovable—the expression of compassion, mercy, and grace in the midst of the world. They would describe it as a Christlikeness that is willing to befriend the kind of people that Jesus befriended. I think they would describe it

as a "loving of the enemy" and a "seeking of reconciliation with the enemy."

After transcribing his holiness sermon "These Brothers and Sisters of Mine," I asked Dr. Ron Benefiel, professor of theology at Point Loma Nazarene University and recent past president of Nazarene Theological Seminary, a similar question: "What does the Wesleyan-Holiness message have to say about human need?" He responded,

> In looking back at our tradition to Wesley and Bresee, I have come to deeply believe that compassion or caring for the poor is not an addendum to our theology of ministry. It's very much tied to holiness, especially the holy character of God. God is holy not only in purity but also in love and compassion, mercy and justice. As the people of God are transformed by the power of God, by the grace of God, and are re-created in God's image, they bear God's holy character in the world. God's love in and through them is a love that engages the world not just in moral purity but also in compassion, mercy and justice.

These pastor/preachers are advancing the heart of Wesley's communities of holiness and compassion. There is no longer a need to explain or justify compassion and justice ministries. If anything, lack of response needs explaining.

In these sermons and conversations with holiness preachers I heard the beginning of a new chapter, if not a new story in the narrative of the Wesleyan-Holiness movement, encapsulated in the phrase "journey inward, journey outward."

Conclusion

The Journey Inward

We know that within Wesleyan-Holiness tradition the inner spiritual life has always been primary even though expressed differently. In her *Theology of Love,* Mildred Wynkoop tried to correct some of what she considered misunderstandings of holiness that crept in during the nineteenth and early twentieth centuries. In his book *A Century of Holiness Theology: The Doctrine of Entire Sanctification in the Church of the Nazarene: 1905 to 2004,* Mark Quanstrom documented the variety of holiness definitions developed during the nineteenth and twentieth centuries.[19] The holiness message is evolving around the central theme of perfect love, an experience and practice of inner spirituality. However it is understood or misunderstood, it has always been about an intentional inward spiritual life beyond a basic affirmation of Christian doctrine.

Upon joining a Church of the Saviour mission group, for the first time in my life I became accountable to a spiritual director for spiritual practices similar to those in Wesley's Methodist classes and bands. For Wesley, sanctification or holiness was more than an individual religious experience. Holiness, as demonstrated by his life and his Methodist followers, was a practice of spiritual development in community. The inward journey is complementary to the outward journey. Neither is complete without the other.

The Journey Outward

For Wesley and the founders of the Church of the Nazarene, holiness was also the practice of compassion, mercy, and justice.

Holiness in this tradition is more than a private experience; it is a way of living in communities of compassion and hospitality reaching out to and welcoming the poor and disinherited. It is a life of compassion inspired by the biblical understanding of perfect love of God and neighbor. The practice of holiness or sanctification is a journey to and with God. God is known in practices of contemplation, prayer, and silence. And God is encountered in the outward journey as well, as in Mother Teresa's words—"Jesus comes to us in the distressing disguise of the poor."

To fully recover the practice of holiness as a life of compassion we need a new story, a new way of understanding an ancient Christian tradition that predates even Wesley and Bresee. Thus I have come to embrace the simple phrase "journey inward, journey outward" from the title of Elizabeth O'Connor's book as a brief description of the practice of holiness. Perhaps it could be a way of rewriting the story that is in keeping with the tradition while also motivating us to practice holiness—inwardly and outwardly.

The idea of writing a new story occurred during a recent meeting including Abdul Aziz Said and after reading his book *Islam and Peacemaking in the Middle East*.[20] As a Syrian-American, he has been teaching at American University in Washington, D.C., since 1957. He is the senior ranking professor of international relations at AU and is the founder of the Center for Global Peace.

In the second chapter of his book, titled "The Need for a New Story," Said writes that Middle East peace will come only when the "confrontational story" or stories are replaced with a "compatibility story." I suggest the phrase "journey inward, journey outward" as the theme of a new holiness "compatibility story" of spirituality in a life of compassion.

In this story, we would recognize that holiness is a practice of both inner spirituality and a compassionate life among those within and outside our faith communities. We would recognize that the inward journey of holiness might take many routes regardless of where it begins. We would be willing to let go of our confrontation stories with their legalisms and exclusive claims to truth. We would reject the confrontation story of fundamentalism. As professor Said writes: "Fundamentalism implies a refusal to listen to the 'other.'" We would recognize that holiness is a practice of compassion and hospitality, leading us outward to a world of suffering and human need.

In our compatibility story we would respond to human suffering wherever it exists and cease our disputes about the social gospel and social justice. We would recognize that evangelism—sharing the good news—is always compassionate and that Christian compassion *is* the good news or evangelism. The new holiness compatibility story is, to coin a phrase, compassion/evangelism.

I believe this theme and story will be well received beyond the boundaries of our own tribe. Evidently, the increasing number of "nones," those claiming no religious affiliation, is not a reaction to spirituality and compassion but to the old stories of religious disputes, contentious true believers, and indifference to a world of need. We can connect with even the "nones" by telling the new holiness story as an intentional journey of spirituality and compassion. With this new story we can retain and attract the next generation as we recover and are faithful to our own tradition.

As in the subtitle of Jonah Sachs' recent book, *Winning the Story Wars,*[21] "Those who tell—and live—the best stories will rule the future." "Journey outward, journey inward" is our story. The future may well belong to those who tell—and live—it.

· · · · · · · · · · · · ·

TOM NEES, **formerly director of the USA/Canada Mission/Evangelism Department for the Church of the Nazarene, now serves as president of Leading to Serve (www.leadingtoserve.com), an organization dedicated to leadership and mentor training.**

two

SHALOM
The End of Holiness

Timothy M. Green

● ●

The biblical call to the people of God is consistent and clear: "You shall be holy, for I the LORD your God am holy" (Lev. 19:2).* "Pursue peace with everyone, and the holiness without which no one will see the Lord" (Heb. 12:14). "May he so strengthen your hearts in holiness that you may be blameless before our God and Father at the coming of our Lord Jesus with all his saints. . . . For God did not call us to impurity but in holiness" (1 Thess. 3:13; 4:7).

In spite of the repeated failures of the Lord's covenant people, first ancient Israel and then the church, to be holy and to embody holiness, even the most simplistic reading of Scripture affirms God's repeated call to his people that they be holy. The question that confronts us, therefore, is not "Does Christian Scripture call the people of God to holiness?" Rather the question that challenges us regarding biblical holiness is embodied

---

*All Scripture quotations in this chapter are from the *New Revised Standard Version* (NRSV) of the Bible.

in the familiar one-word inquiry raised by the curious child: "Why?" Why would God call the people with whom he shares covenant to *be* a holy people and to embody that *being* through their lives together and in the world? While articulations, explanations, and even vocabulary of both the "what" and the "how" of holiness may vary in our Christian Scripture and tradition, *why* do both Scripture and tradition affirm God's concern for his people to be a holy people? What is the purpose, the reason, the *telos* of holiness? In other words, what is the *end* of holiness?

The question regarding the end of holiness is directly related to the much larger question concerning the purpose of God's people in relationship to the nations and to creation itself. The question expands even more broadly to the purpose or end of human beings in relationship to God, to creation, and to other humans. In the broadest of contexts, these questions point to the ultimate question regarding the ultimate end to which God is intending to take all creation.

In order to explore this question of "why" or "to what end," we will turn our attention to one particular theological voice that is woven throughout our Christian Scripture. We will refer to this theological voice as the *priestly voice.* Of the various theological voices in Christian Scripture, the voice of the priests provides the most clear, direct, and consistent call upon the people of God both to *be* holy and to *embody* a life of holiness. This theological voice not only calls the people to holiness but also grounds the call to holiness in the reason for the existence of God's covenant people, the nature of the human race as the image of God, and ultimately in the overarching purpose of God for creation itself. This theological voice calls the people of God to holiness as well as seeks to respond to that perennial childlike question, "Why?" Therefore, we will turn our attention to this unique voice in our Scripture as we attempt to envision the *end* of holiness.

The Priestly Voice in the Old Testament

It is the priestly voice that provides us with the classic injunction, "You shall be holy, for I the Lord your God am holy" (Lev. 19:2). The priestly theological handbook from which this call emerges, Leviticus, concerns itself with articulating the life of holiness in everyday affairs, from diet to discharges, from sacrifice to sexuality. It reaches its crescendo in Leviticus 19 as it associates the call to the covenant community to be holy with the holiness of God (v. 2). In this chapter, admonitions to show reverence for one's parents, to observe Sabbath, to leave the edges of a harvested field for the poor, to refrain from exercising fraud, and to abstain from harassing the deaf and the blind reach their climax in the declaration, "You shall not take vengeance or bear a grudge against any of your people, but you shall love your neighbor as yourself: I am the Lord" (v. 18).

The convictions of this theological voice provide the framework for the great narrative that begins in Genesis and continues through Numbers. This narrative incorporates the depiction of creation, the promise to Abraham, the liberation from captivity, the covenant at Sinai, the construction of the tabernacle, and the repeated failures of the people of God to trust their covenant-making God. The priestly distinctions between clean and unclean, holy and unholy and the relationship of these distinctions to the glory-bearing temple of the Lord in Jerusalem culminate in the messages of Ezekiel. Taken together, the "theological handbook" of Leviticus, the extended narrative of Genesis—Numbers, and the proclamation of Ezekiel provide us with the theological vision of the priestly voice.

The priestly voice particularly emphasizes the distinct uniqueness, "set apartness," or holiness of the Lord (Yahweh) God from all other powers, both divine and human. This theological voice directly associates the distinctive otherness of the Lord God with the necessary nature and character of the community with whom the Lord God has initiated a covenant. They understood that a people in covenant with such a uniquely distinct (i.e., holy) God must itself be uniquely distinct (i.e., holy) in relationship to all other nations and communities. The priestly voice was insistent that the uniqueness of the covenant community among the peoples of the earth was directly linked to the uniqueness of the God with whom it shared covenant. As their God was uniquely set apart from all other divine and earthly powers, so they were to be uniquely set apart from the nations of the world. They were somehow to embody the *difference* of their covenant God.

But to this priestly emphasis upon *difference*, uniqueness, or holiness, we are compelled to ask, "Why?" Were they to be set apart simply to proverbially *stand out from the rest*? Distinct for the sake of distinctiveness? Is that the ultimate end? Were they to be odd for the sake of oddity? Is that the final *telos*? What is the purpose of this uniqueness, "set apartness," holiness? What is its end? As we explore the interlocking convictions that inform the concerns of the priestly theological handbook of Leviticus, the narratives written in Genesis—Numbers, and the proclamation of Ezekiel, we begin to discover the "why" concerning the priestly call to holiness. Akin to the child's dot-to-dot drawing, one conviction interfaces with the next, and only in the totality of the "dots" does the fuller priestly portrait begin to emerge. As any one of these convictions is not present, the fuller priestly vision of God, creation, God's covenant people, and the divine call to holiness evaporates. However, as we "connect the dots" of these convictions and perceive their interrelatedness, we might begin to comprehend the overarching priestly vision of God, God's creation, the covenant people, and the call to holiness. Let's proceed to explore briefly four key convictions that inform the priestly theological vision and ultimately serve to inform a biblical understanding of the end of holiness.

Guiding Priestly Convictions

(1) **God is up to something.** At the very core of priestly thought is the guiding conviction that God continues to be actively engaged in his world. The priests affirm that God not only initiated his divine agenda in creation but that he *continues* to engage in carrying out that divine agenda. For the priestly voice, the divine agenda of creation is both an initial divine activity and an ongoing divine activity. From the priestly perspective, the divine actions of creation are the demonstrations of God's will for life.

As recounted in the opening narrative of the priestly voice in Genesis 1, from the very beginning God has been making room for life. Where there are potential threats to life and where barrenness is present (i.e., darkness and chaotic waters), God overcomes the threat to life. He proceeds to provide the context in which life not only will exist but will thrive. He then brings forth life and proceeds to empower that life to continue to engender life, to *be fruitful and multiply.*

In the minds of the priests, this life-giving, life-sustaining, and life-empowering activity is the divine agenda. Life-threatening darkness and chaotic waters are overcome through divine "dividing," whether that divine action be in God's life-giving acts of creation in Genesis 1 or in God's later life-giving, redemptive/creative acts of deliverance out of Egypt and across the Sea. No wonder, the recurring biblical images of that which threatens life are darkness and chaotic waters (from repeated outcries concerning darkness and drowning waters in the Psalms to the repeated miraculous healings of blind people and calming of stormy seas by Jesus). It comes as no surprise that the Revelator imagines a tomorrow void of threats to life: no Sea and no night (Rev. 21:1; 22:5).

Having properly ordered the cosmos in the seven days of Genesis 1, God proceeds to carry out the divine "agenda of life" in Genesis 2 by properly ordering human relationships with God, with creation, and with other human beings. As life becomes *disordered* through the exercise of abusive power and violence by human beings in Genesis 3—4, these same divinely ordered relationships deteriorate. Ultimately those that were intended by God to be life-giving, trusting relationships become life-taking, mistrusting relationships (3:14-19; 4:10-14).

The first convictional "dot" in the matrix of the priestly voice is God's agenda of life. Where there is barrenness, blessing. Where there is darkness, light. Where there is disease, well-being. Where there is brokenness, completeness. Where there is violence, peace. Where there is fear, trust. Where there is hopelessness, hope. Where there is alienation, reconciliation. Where there is isolation, properly ordered relationships. For the priests and for that matter for the multiplicity of theological voices in Scripture, life, blessing, well-being, completeness, peace, trust, hope, reconciliation, and properly ordered relationships can be captured in a single word: *shalom*. No wonder, the great priestly benediction found in Numbers 6:24-26 concludes with the prayer: "The LORD lift up his countenance upon you, and give you [*shalom*]."

(2) **God is not a micromanager.** The second convictional "dot" directly connected to the first concerns the nature of the

Lord God whose agenda is life. In contrast to the other deities of the ancient world, including Zeus who sits stoically atop Mount Olympus, the creative sovereignty of the Lord God is not expressed through manipulative, "micromanaging" activities. Rather the God of Christian Scripture vulnerably yet daringly opens himself to the cooperative "partnership" with his creation.

As the priests recount the story of God's creative activity in Genesis 1, they undoubtedly present God as the initiator of all life-giving activity. He creates the light, but then he uses the light to divide the darkness. He creates the firmament, but he proceeds to use the firmament to divide the waters. In like manner, he calls for the land to produce vegetation, the waters to send forth fish, and the land to bring forth animals. He entrusts the rule of the day to the sun and the rule of the night to the moon. And as if all of these divinely initiated "partnerships" were not enough, God ultimately creates his image, the human race, to fill the land, to domesticate it, and to exercise protective custody over every living thing.

The priests dared to believe that their sovereign God, the Lord whom they worshipped and of whom they instructed others in his ways, is no self-serving despot who uses sovereign power in manipulative and controlling ways. He is no mistrusting, skeptical, micromanaging deity. Rather he willingly entrusts, he vulnerably believes in, and he boldly enters into an authentic relationship with his creation, particularly a relationship with his own image, the human race. Just as an image of a deity within an ancient temple pointed away from itself to the deity who is worshipped in that temple, so the priests understood humanity's God-given task to be pointing away from itself to the God who is worshipped in the temple of God's creation. As articulated in the Westminster Catechism, "Man's chief end is to glorify God, and to enjoy him forever."

In summary of the interrelatedness of the first two priestly convictions: while insisting that the Lord God was actively engaged in the life-giving agenda of creation/redemption, the priests were likewise convinced that the Lord's sovereignty was not expressed through unilateral, micromanaging actions but rather through the divine invitation to his creation and particularly to humanity as his image in the world to join him in his creative, life-giving, redeeming work. The divine purpose or end of creation/redemption was life, completeness, well-being, peace, trust, hope, reconciliation, and properly ordered relationships. In other words, *shalom*. And the priests boldly and daringly believed that this God now opened himself to "the other" toward that same end: *shalom*.

(3) **God has committed God's self to a partnership with a unique community to join him in the divine agenda.** While the priestly voice understood the Lord as a nonmicromanaging deity who invited all of humanity and creation itself to participate with him in his creative, redemptive, life-giving agenda, it particularly understood the Lord as entering into a unique relationship of reciprocity with a unique community, Israel. The Lord himself had initiated this relationship by uniquely acting as the divine deliverer-redeemer and provider. Subsequently, he had initiated a covenant with the community whom he had delivered. Although the community was to respond in unadulterated fidelity to its covenant God, divine action preceded human response. The covenant community's obedience was subsequent to divine grace.

Nevertheless, this relationship of covenant was not merely one of an overlord who forced himself upon a mindless subordinate. The relationship of covenant was a bilateral (i.e., two-way street) partnership between God and people. It was most clearly articulated in the covenant formula *I will be your God, and you will be my people* (e.g., see Exod. 6:7). The priests dared to believe that their creating/redeeming yet nonmicromanaging covenant God had called into existence a unique community that would expressly become the Lord's instrument of his gracious continuing creative, redemptive, life-giving work. He had called them into a unique Creator-creature "partnership" with a single end in mind: *shalom.*

Perhaps the most vivid image used by the priests to depict the role of the covenant community emerged from the priests' own identity and role within the community. Just as they were "set apart" from the rest of God's people to carry out such priestly tasks as instructing the community in God's will, offering sacrifices on behalf of the community, and speaking blessing upon the community, so too was the covenant community to carry out the priestly life-giving tasks on behalf of the nations and for the sake of all creation. The people of God were to be a "set apart people" (i.e., holy nation) *from the world* in order to serve as a "community of priests" (i.e., priestly kingdom) *for the sake of the world*. The priests clearly affirmed, "Indeed, the whole earth is mine, but you shall be for me a priestly kingdom and a holy nation" (Exod. 19:6).

The call placed upon the covenant community to be a holy people served the greater *end* of their being priests set apart for the sake of the world, set apart in order to cooperate with their covenant God in his creative, redemptive, life-giving agenda. The priests refused to separate the call to holiness from the divine mission in which the covenant community was now participating. The people's unique, even "set apart," nature (i.e., holiness) was not the end in itself. For the priests, their "set apartness" served a much greater end: the divine agenda of *shalom.*

Looking back to the inception of God's people, the people's priestly role fulfilled the promise that God had made to Abram and Sarai: "I will bless you . . . so that you will be a blessing . . . and in you all the families of the earth shall be blessed" (Gen. 12:2-3). Just as God had pronounced the blessing of life upon creation and the human race at the beginning of his creative work (see Gen. 1:22, 28; *Be fruitful and multiply*), God placed the blessing of life upon this nomadic man and barren woman so that they might become God's instruments of life-giving blessing to the world. In other words, they were blessed to become a blessing. Graced by the life-giving blessing of God, the covenant community would become the means of God's gracious, life-giving blessing to the world. Like the priests, this community would partner with the Lord in placing the priestly blessing upon the world:

The LORD bless you and keep you;
the LORD make his face to shine upon you, and be gracious
    to you;
the LORD lift up his countenance upon you, and give you
    peace [*shalom*]. (Num. 6:24-26)

Imitating their covenant God who had refused to curse the darkness at creation but spoke light into that darkness, the covenant community was called not to curse the abyss of human depravity, brokenness, and violence but to "light a candle in the darkness" and speak *shalom*.

In addition to the images of priestly kingdom and blessing, a third image is used by the priests to describe the covenant community's cooperative "partnership" with God's agenda of life-giving creation/redemption. As the people of God bear the tabernacle throughout their journey, they become the "glory-bearers" of the tabernacling presence of God in the world. They become the community "set apart" to bear that which sets the Lord apart from all other powers, both human and divine. Refusing to remain behind at Mount Sinai, the Lord God journeys with his people and in so doing his people bear the unique nature, the "otherness," of their God.

So what is that glory? How might one describe it? What is this "otherness" that makes the Lord God distinct from all other powers and authorities, both divine and human? As the unseen divine glory passes by Moses, the Lord articulates the nature of his glory: "The LORD, the LORD, a God merciful and gracious, slow to anger, and abounding in steadfast love and faithfulness, keeping steadfast love for the thousandth generation, forgiving iniquity and transgression and sin" (Exod. 34:6-7). The unmatchable, unique, "holy" glory of God that tabernacles with and through the covenant people of God is this: mercy, grace, slowness to anger, abundant love and fidelity, forgiveness. Just imagine what it might look like for the community of God's people to bear that divine glory! No wonder the glory-bearing community is called to be distinct or set apart from the nations; no God and no nation had ever been described in such a unique way.

(4) **The human dilemma and the divine stubborn refusal.** A fourth and final "dot" is necessary if we are to envision the complete priestly picture of God, his people, and the divine call to and purpose of holiness. The priestly voice was most certainly aware of the nagging, perennial problem of the covenant people. As the community set part to bear the divine glory, they were called to be unique or holy. Yet generation after generation, the people of God succumbed to allegiances with other powers and authorities, sometimes religious and sometimes political. Taking on the personalities of the imperial and religious powers, the people of God engaged in violence, sometimes physical, other times economic, and other times judicial. Yet they habitually engaged in the violent, life-taking activities

of the dominant culture rather than the life-giving, *shalom*-oriented agenda of God.

In spite of the habitual pattern of God's people, the priests dared to believe that their covenant-making, nonmicromanaging, creating/redeeming God refused to surrender to his people's failures. He would neither forsake his covenant partner nor compromise the divine call to holiness. The priestly voice tenaciously held on to the hope that the God who had called his people to be his instruments set apart for divine blessing to all nations and to creation itself would graciously act in such a way that his people would faithfully carry out their priestly calling in the world.

No priestly voice is any clearer on this divine commitment than Ezekiel. Idolatry and violence had consumed the people of God; it had infiltrated both their temple and their society (see Ezek. 8). As a result, they were incapable of being the people set apart to bear the divine uniqueness in the world. Thus, that uniqueness—the divine glory—must depart (10:18-19). However, this departure only sets the stage for the divinely initiated and gracious act in which the glory would ultimately return. In the end, Ezekiel envisions the utter transformation by God himself of people, temple, and land. As a result of such transformation, the covenant community would ultimately fulfill the end to which it was called. They would become the authentic, divine instrument set apart by God in order that God's life-giving agenda of *shalom* might be carried out for the sake of the world.

According to Ezekiel, this gracious transformation would not be for the sake of the covenant people but would be for the sake of God's own name (i.e., reputation). In order for the divine name to be appropriately embodied, the name-bearers (glory-bearers) must be transformed (see chap. 36): purging of idols, willing heart, the life-giving Spirit of God. In signifying the interconnectedness between God and his people, the Lord announces, "I will sanctify [*make holy*] my great name . . . when through you I display my holiness before their [*the nations'*] eyes" (36:23). What the people were unable to do in their own effort, the Lord would do by grace.

And why? What results from this divine action of *making holy*? The people, the land, and the temple would all be restored to their original calling: life-giving instruments of *shalom*. In a concluding vision, Ezekiel imagines fresh, life-giving water that flows out from the four corners of the transformed temple to the most lifeless, hopeless, barren, deathly, forsaken, fear-filled places on earth (chap. 47). As it grows deeper and reaches the deadliest places on earth, life, hope, fertility, resurrection, reconciliation, and trust abound. Imagine that . . . the most deadly sea becomes lined with fruit-bearing trees and filled with fish. The *end* of holiness has come as the people of God by the grace of God have become cooperators with God as they live into God's life-filled, hope-filled future of *shalom*. Certainly, the life envisioned is not the result of clever human maneuvers; life emerges only because "The LORD is There" (48:35). Just think about it: death does not overcome life, but life overcomes death. In the end, the unholy does not contaminate the holy, but the holy contagiously affects and transforms the unholy. Behold, all things become new. And the end of God's creative/redemptive mission, the end of the cooperative mission of the people of God, ah, indeed, the end of holiness has become a reality: *Your kingdom come. Your will be done, on earth as it is in heaven* (Matt. 6:10) . . . *shalom!*

Where Do We Go from Here?

So what is the end of holiness? The simple yet profound convictions that guide the priestly vision lead us into at least one consistent biblical response to that question: God is up to something, the life-giving agenda of *shalom*. Yet he is no micromanaging deity, and he has called into existence a unique partner to be his priestly kingdom, means of gracious blessing, glory-bearing community among whom the tabernacling presence of God is uniquely evident. Although God's covenant partner perpetually struggles to embody faithfully its cooperative identity and task, the Lord refuses to abandon his life-giving agenda, his nonmicromanaging nature, and the community with whom he has made a unique covenant. With divine resoluteness and by his own gracious initiative, he will act for the sake of his name—his mission, his nature, his people. He will make his name holy by making his people holy. He is resolute that his people will faithfully *be* his people in the world and will faithfully *carry out* the priestly task with which he has entrusted them. Holiness with a purpose, an end: to enter into and participate faithfully with God in the brokenness of life as a means of God's life-giving grace. Light in darkness; wholeness in brokenness; life in deathliness; hope in hopelessness. *Shalom*.

Perhaps one of the most appropriate prayers for the kingdom of priests—the church (1 Pet. 2:9)—to pray with "the end" of holiness in mind is the prayer commonly attributed to Francis of Assisi:

Lord, make me an instrument of your peace [*shalom*].
Where there is hatred, let me sow love;
Where there is injury, pardon;
Where there is doubt, faith;
Where there is despair, hope;
Where there is darkness, light;

Where there is sadness, joy.

O Divine Master, grant that I may not so much seek
To be consoled as to console,
To be understood as to understand,
To be loved as to love.
For it is in giving that we receive;
It is in pardoning that we are pardoned;
It is in dying that we are born to eternal life.

By the grace of God, may the end of holiness be realized in our lives and in the life of Christ's church. Indeed, may "your kingdom come. Your will be done, on earth as it is in heaven." *Shalom.*

• • • • • • • • • • • • • •

TIMOTHY M. GREEN **is professor of Old Testament at Trevecca Nazarene University, where he also serves as university chaplain and
dean of the School of Theology and Christian Ministry.**

three

THY KINGDOM COME
HOLINESS AND THE NEW CREATION

Carl M. Leth

Introduction

Why should we choose a study of holiness as a context for a discussion of compassion and ministries of compassion? I suspect that more than a few folks thought this question after reading the title of this book. Aren't these two different conversations separate, if not competing? From the beginnings of the resurgence of concern for compassionate ministry in the 1970s—and since then—a recurring perspective on compassionate ministry has been concern that an active focus on compassion would distract us from our central mission of holiness and evangelism, perhaps even supplanting that central focus on holiness with a social reform agenda, a social gospel. For the sake of good works in our society do we risk losing focus on the primary work of the kingdom?

The prospect that a holiness conference on compassion might prompt this kind of concern is precisely the reason we need to reconsider our understanding of the relation of holiness and compassion. What is the place of compassion in the life of holiness?

Holiness and Compassion in Context

To properly understand holiness and compassion we need to reconsider the broader context—our understanding of soteriology. What is centrally at stake in this conversation is our understanding of the nature and scope of God's work of salvation—his work of redemption. How we understand the redemptive work of God defines our understanding of holiness and the place of compassion in the holy life. By holiness here I am not merely referring to entire sanctification but to the broader vision of God's restorative work in which entire sanctification is an important component. What is it that God is doing?

It is here that we come to the problem of the "pottage diet." I want to propose a change in diet, theologically speaking, as the way forward in considering the place of compassion in the holy life. It concerns the "pottage diet." I am not proposing that we adopt a diet of pottage, but that we choose a diet that abandons pottage. Just as Esau surrendered his birthright to satisfy the insistent demands of his hunger, so we risk surrendering the fullness of our heritage in response to the insistent demands of contemporary conversations or trends. The metaphorical "pottage" I am so anxious to abandon is the popular soteriology of modern reformed evangelicalism that has influenced us so significantly—to our detriment.

In consideration of the place of compassion in the holy life, the way forward is not to abandon our heritage or to substantively revision it, but to more faithfully reclaim it. Like Esau we have been enticed by the vision of salvation made so conveniently available to us, inclining us increasingly to abandon the richer birthright that should be ours. We have too often and too extensively accepted the thin gruel of modern reformed evangelicalism and its soteriological agenda. We have feasted on the pottage served us and left the robust legacy of our tradition—at its best—behind. As a result we have accommodated ourselves to a reductionist understanding of salvation and holiness, a meager vision of God's work of redemption.

The roots of this dilemma stretch back to the Reformation. Martin Luther, in his concern to radically separate human contributions to our salvation from salvation by grace alone, separated our justification before God and our regeneration and transformation into his likeness. We become righteous before God—hidden behind the atoning righteousness of Christ—but remain sinners in fact. His concern was to free us from any bondage of works as a prerequisite to our justification, but the result was a sharp disjunction between justification and regeneration, the forensic (legal) and therapeutic (transformational) aspects of salvation.

This is a disjunction that John Wesley emphatically rejected. Our justification before God and our regeneration into his likeness may be logically distinguished but are inextricable in human experience. They are two aspects of one redemptive work. To come to Christ is to be changed. We are justified by grace alone, but we are also transformed by that same grace. To become Christian is to be made holy.

It is this disjunction between justification and regeneration or sanctification that sets a trajectory that extends into contemporary evangelicalism. It gives birth to a soteriology that is both gnostic and individualistic in disposition, if not in fact. That is, it encourages an understanding of salvation that radically separates salvation (as resolution of a spiritual reality) from regeneration or sanctification (as transformation of a lived reality). As a result, life lived in the flesh—as an aspect of our salvation—is diminished in significance, sometimes to the point of irrelevance. It also focuses on a soteriology that concerns the individual primarily, perhaps essentially. The limiting scope of redemption is salvation of individual persons. Together these define in significant, and limiting, ways the nature and scope of salvation.

The Nature of Salvation

Let's consider first the nature of salvation. A soteriology that moves the critical issue of salvation to a spiritual realm, leaving the matter of change of life to a subsequent and secondary consideration suggests a gnostic predisposition, devaluing life in the flesh in preference for a spiritualized (disembodied) understanding of life. It is gnostic because it is primarily concerned with a spiritual disposition (especially after death) and only secondarily concerned with salvation as a changed incarnational reality. Salvation becomes—at its most basic understanding—a ticket to heaven, concerned fundamentally with our destiny beyond this life but not with our conduct in this life.

Justification—as a spiritual reality—is, at best, separated from regeneration as a subsequent (and, therefore, secondary) concern and, at worst, makes change of life essentially irrelevant to our salvation. It is this logical extension that provides the theological rationale for current popular notions of salvation and eternal security without any necessity for change of life. My confidence in my eternal salvation and the transformation of my living become two different—and separate—conversations. I can claim salvation without any necessary expectation of regeneration or sanctification.

It is high time we reject the limitations of this vision of soteriology. It is small wonder that within Reformed evangelicalism today there is an energetic, sometimes strident, debate about the adequacy of this soteriology. It is one of the driving issues motivating the emerging church movement, which is dominantly a product of dissatisfaction with Reformed evangelicalism. While I wish our Reformed evangelical brothers and sisters well in their ongoing conversation, I want to call the Wesleyan-Holiness community away from that conversation to engage instead in a constructive dialogue with our own tradition.

I am not proposing that we idealize our tradition. I am well aware of the particular failings of our tradition. And we need to take them seriously. But I *am* proposing that when we consider our tradition at its best we discover a rich resource for a robust soteriology. It is in the context of that robust soteriology that we can find the place of compassion in the life of holiness.

Here, in contrast to the watery pottage of contemporary evangelicalism, we discover a vigorously incarnational soteriology. Wesley's rejection of justification essentially separated from regeneration and sanctification reflects a fundamental and emphatic commitment to the expectation of transformation as essentially connected to God's work of redemption. New birth, regeneration, and sanctification are inseparably linked to God's saving work. This is not a merely abstract affirmation. It is a profoundly incarnational understanding of redemption. Salvation is, and must be, a life-changing reality.

Salvation surely includes the expectation of heaven as a future reality. I embrace and celebrate that eschatological expectation. But our vision of salvation also includes the expectation of heaven breaking into this present reality, an inaugurated eschatology that is present as well as future. Salvation involves participation in that transforming reality now—in this life—as well as expectation of its ultimate realization. Our traditional history, even when it includes some more embarrassing episodes, serves to underscore this profound commitment. Becoming a Christian in the holiness tradition meant that life must be radically changed.

- the cigarettes were left on the altar
- the liquor bottles went out with the trash
- make-up came off
- we let our women's hair grow long
- the cinema became off-limits
- we didn't dance and we didn't chew
- we took axes to our TVs

I'm not proposing that all of these practices and so many like them should be uncritically reclaimed. But we should recognize in them a radical commitment to a changed life—in every respect—as a consequence of choosing to follow Jesus. To be saved meant that life—in the flesh—was changed. To be being made holy implied thoroughly transformed living.

Salvation was no mere spiritual event, but a radically transforming incarnational reality. Dietrich Bonhoeffer's lament concerning "cheap grace" might resonate with the inheritors of Luther's soteriological vision but would be an "alien righteousness" to folks in the holiness tradition. Our experience of saving grace was never "cheap," but rigorously engaging and thoroughly transforming—everything changed. The secondness of entire sanctification was not primarily about the chronology of human experience but a claim concerning the scope of transformation expected in this life.

So, let us consider the nature of redemption reclaimed from our tradition. Salvation is a thoroughly transforming incarnational reality, beginning when we accept Christ and extending across life into eternity. It encompasses every aspect of life, calling us to live as followers of Christ, becoming like him. Being Christian entails radical commitment to kingdom living.

This must certainly include living lives of compassion. The reordered disposition of heart and life turns us toward God and neighbor. Love of God and love of neighbor are inseparable. To love God is also to love as—and who—God loves. God's heart of compassion—so clearly evident in the biblical record—becomes the forming pattern for our hearts. That new heart of compassion issues into a life of compassion. This is not an elective addition to salvation, but an essential product and evidence of salvation.

God defines his attitude and relation to humanity in the incarnation. God "bends down" to humanity, giving himself to and for them. The incarnation reveals the reality of God's life and character as Christ "empties himself" for the sake of sinful, broken humankind—he "bends down" to sinners. To be like him, to be restored into his image, must include "bending down" as Christ bends down. As God's heart moves out in Christ, so our hearts—and lives—must move out to others as we reflect his life. Any Christian life that does less fails to faithfully reflect the God who reveals himself to us in Christ.

The Scope of Salvation

There is a further step in our reappropriation of the best our tradition offers us. That is consideration of the scope of redemption. For the inherited soteriology of Reformed evangelicalism salvation is primarily, even exclusively, individual. It is our personal spiritual destiny that is in view. While our tradition deeply values the importance of personal salvation, it also calls us to a broader vision of the scope of God's redemptive work.

Please understand me carefully here. I am not proposing a rejection or replacement of a vision of personal salvation, nor do I want to minimize the significance of decisive personal moments in our experience and realization of God's work of redemption in us. I affirm and celebrate this reality. Rather, what I want to suggest is that we will most appropriately and adequately understand and value those personal realities when we understand them in the context of God's greater work of redemption. Our personal salvation is a central part of God's redeeming work, but it is not the whole work.

The kingdom of God that Jesus declared to be present brings a comprehensive vision of restoration. The work that God has already begun is moving to a completion when all will be re-ordered in right relation under the rule of God. The disorder of sin will be healed—in every respect. God's restoration of our lives individually is part of a greater work in which all of creation is being—and will be—restored.

Wesley draws on the biblical language of new creation. The reality of that in-breaking new creation promises personal restoration and transformation. It envisions a thoroughly incarnational redemption. But because that incarnational reality is both personal and communal it also envisions social restoration. That restoration involves our relations with others in the church. Christianity takes place, for Wesley, in the context of Christian community. Wesley's oft-cited "There is no holiness but social holiness" is a reference to holiness being realized in community, the fellowship of the church. It is here that holiness happens. Our community, in Christ, is the realization and context for the reality of the new creation.

It also includes the concern of Christians in community for those in need, the practice of compassion moving to love the neighbor. Wesley's early Methodists were called to regular, personal interaction with the poor. His emphatic call to (what we would name as) "ministries of compassion" were expected to be an integral part of the transformed reality of those who were being transformed by the new creation. They were a means of grace—both to the poor and to the Christian ministering to the poor. Compassion was not a distraction from deepening discipleship but a needful element contributing to it. It was part of becoming holy.

Wesley's vision of the new creation also includes the restoration of broader social realities and political systems. The patterns and systems of this sinful world will be reordered by this in-breaking reality. To be Christian is to be engaged in this transforming work. This concern would even include the material world, God's natural creation that "groans" in anticipation of Christ's redemption and restoration. All of the creation that sin has disordered will be made whole and restored—the realization of shalom, the end of holiness. Living the life of holiness, then, goes beyond internal personal piety (as important as that is) to include our embodied engagement in God's comprehensive work of the new creation.

This insight was assumed by the early Methodists and the Holiness Movement in the United States. Holiness people were actively involved in opposition to slavery and advocacy for the status of women. The "Free" in Free Methodist was originally driven, at least in part, by their committed opposition to slavery. Women were ordained and validated as full partners in ministry in the Holiness Movement long before the role of women in ministry came on the radar of liberal Protestantism. The holiness folks created missions in the centers of distressed urban areas and established homes for marginalized unwed mothers across the country. Educational institutions were formed everywhere holiness people gathered, as an extension of the mission of holiness.

Holiness moved them into the world, not to reform it, but to transform it, into the reality of God's new creation. This is evident even in the particular legalism of the later Holiness Movement. I am old enough to recall exhortations to avoid the cinema, not only to escape personal immorality but also to boycott the culture and institutions of Hollywood, to avoid supporting systems of social disorder. These, too, were called under the transforming judgment of the kingdom of God and its new creation. Systems of sin as well as individual acts of sin were called into judgment and the corrective, reordering reality of the kingdom of God.

Holiness and Compassion

We come, at last, to the specific question of the place of compassion in the holy life. In the context of a reconsidered soteriology we find that compassion is not only congenial but also essential to the life of holiness. To participate in the incarnational reality of kingdom life must essentially include love of neighbor as an extension of our love of God. To be reordered by the rule and character of God is to be moved by what moves him, to be drawn to participate in what he does. In other words, to propose a holy life that is *not* essentially concerned with compassion is a contradiction in terms. Further, the concern for compassion in the holy life cannot be limited to merely internal or personal attitudes or dispositions. It must be essentially incarnational, engaged in the transformation of life, and in the larger scope of God's redemption—the new creation.

Understanding compassion in the context of this reconsidered soteriology not only suggests the necessity of compassion but also demands that we define our understanding of the character of compassion in terms of this soteriology. This is not a compassion that is shaped and driven by economic models or political ideologies. This is, rather, a compassion that emerges naturally from an understanding and experience of holiness.

The life of holiness is moved to a compassion that comes from the character of Christ, is actualized by the Holy Spirit, and envisions restoration into the new creation as the end of compassion.

This means that our ministries of compassion should not be merely palliative but restorative. It is not enough to offer only comfort and relief to the distressed. God's heart of compassion toward them aspires for more—their healing enfolding into the redemptive reality into which he came to invite them. Compassion that is merely compassion—disconnected from the soteriological vision of God's new creation—is minimally redemptive, offering some relief from suffering without offering healing and restoration that may move beyond suffering to wholeness. That means ministries of compassion that envision only economic improvement or relief of immediate need inadequately reflect holiness compassion.

This also suggests that holiness compassion must be necessarily concerned with effect. Acts of kindness or generosity are expressions of piety, but apart from realization of the new creation they are not fully redemptive. Not all charity contributes to the realization of kingdom life. It is not enough that our intentions are generous or noble. The effect of our actions should be healing and restorative for the people receiving our charity. They should be empowered and humanized as a result of our compassion. To act compassionately cannot be sufficient unless our compassionate activity is participating in the in-breaking reality of the kingdom—God's new creation. Toxic charity cannot be true holiness compassion. Holiness compassion must be the heart—and rule—of God breaking into the broken realities of this sinful world to redeem and transform them.

Let me also note an important characteristic of the Wesleyan-Holiness tradition that bears remembering when we consider the challenging ministry of compassion in a world so broken.

That characteristic is the quality of bold expectation. John Wesley and the subsequent Holiness Movement are distinctive in their bold expectation of the realization of the possibilities of holiness in this life. This may be the most distinctively defining characteristic of the Wesleyan-Holiness tradition. All Christian traditions envision the restoration of God's rule and kingdom life at the end of time. For our tradition God's re-creative work is our expectation *in* this life. Our work is done in the confident expectation that with God all things are possible and that he will see this through to completion. Like the heroes of Hebrews 11, we may not see its fulfillment, but we can be confident that the new creation is certainly breaking in now and will bring all things under the rule and reign of God. Our work of compassion is not palliative, easing suffering without hope of healing, but expectant and confident in the power of God to bring the reality of his new creation into the present. Holiness compassion is the kind of compassion that can expect real change in the broken, sinful realities that surround us.

Conclusion

If we revisit the question of choosing to consider compassion in the context of a consideration of holiness, we can now respond that not only is holiness an appropriate context for consideration of compassion, but it is, in fact, the most appropriate context for considering compassion at its best. To be made holy, to be made like God in Christ, essentially includes compassion. To participate in the work of Christ involves, essentially, a heart and life of compassion. God's work of holiness envisions—and actualizes—the restoration of a reality disordered by sin. The optimism of holiness expects the in-breaking reality of that restoration in this life.

This is the robust holiness soteriology that our tradition offers us as a context for understanding and practicing compassion. No thin gruel here. Let me invite you to the feast. Here we find a bold, comprehensive vision—and expectation—of God's work. And at the heart of holiness we find compassion.

• • • • • • • • • • • • • •

CARL M. LETH is dean of the School of Theology and Christian Ministry at Olivet Nazarene University. He also serves as pastor of the Wildwood Church of the Nazarene, a multicultural congregation in downtown Kankakee, Illinois.

four

COVENANT AND COMPASSION

Kevin Mellish

• •

The call to have compassion on those who were socially and economically disadvantaged in Israel's community and to care for their needs reverberates throughout the Old Testament. The prophets frequently encouraged members of the community to come to the aid of the fatherless, the widow, and the stranger while simultaneously levying harsh critiques against those who oppressed and exploited the poor (Isa. 1:16-17; 10:1-2; Jer. 5:26-29; 7:6; Ezek. 18:7-8; Amos 2:6-8; 8:4-6; Mic. 2:1-2). The psalmist extolled the individual who gave generously to those in need (37:25-28) and called the individual "blessed" who considered the poor (41:1-2). Job defended his character before God by citing that his care for the poor was the basis for his righteous and ethical behavior (29:12-16; 31:13-22). Similarly, the writer of Proverbs promoted the idea of helping those who were in need and lauded those who were kind to those living in poverty (14:21; 19:17; 21:13, 16; 23:10-11; 28:8; 31:9, 20). Within the narrative tradition, God established the king to be the instrument of justice and righteousness on earth and to ensure that he "defend the cause of the poor of the people, give deliverance to the needy, and crush the oppressor" (Ps. 72:4).*

These examples highlight the important role that compassion toward the less fortunate played in Israelite thought and belief. Taking care of the economically, politically, and socially vulnerable in society was an integral part of God's covenant relationship with the people of Israel. In order for the Israelites to truly call themselves the people of God, it was imperative that they not only loved and revered God but also demonstrated their love for God by extending mercy, love, and compassion toward their neighbors. The bedrock of Israel's covenant was based upon the Torah, which God gave to Moses after the exodus. It was the Mosaic covenant, and the fundamental principles upon which it was founded, that subsequently inspired the message of the prophets and the other biblical writers on this issue.

The essence of Israel's covenant with God is expressed in the great law codes of Exodus 20—23, Leviticus 1—25, and Deuteronomy 12—26. Here, the basis of God's relationship with the Israelites was spelled out in detail, and God's expectations for Israel were set forth in a covenantal context. Within this covenant tradition, the codes in Exodus and Deuteronomy, in particular, contain the majority of the laws that addressed the plight of the poor and disadvantaged.[1] Taken together, they demonstrate that caring for the poor and needy within the community was central to Israel's identity and mission as the people of God.

Within the book of Exodus, the primary code, known as the Covenant Code (Exod. 20:18—23:19), is prefaced by the Decalogue or the "Ten Words" (20:1-17). Form-critical scholars

---

*Unless otherwise indicated, all Scripture quotations in this chapter are from the *New Revised Standard Version* (NRSV) of the Bible.

have shown that the Decalogue not only shares a relationship with the Covenant Code but contains a logical order as well. The following diagram provides an outline of how the laws in Exodus 20:1-17 are arranged:

Love for God	*Love of Neighbor*
1. No other gods	5. Honor father and mother
2. No idols/images	6. No murder
3. Revering God's name	7. No adultery
4. Sabbath day observance	8. No stealing
	9. No false witness
	10. No coveting

A basic examination of the aforementioned laws reveals that they are predicated on two simple, yet very important ideas. First, Israel was called to love and honor God. This included worshipping Yahweh above all other deities, abstaining from making an idol/image of God, honoring God's name or reputation, and observing the Sabbath as a holy day unto God. The second component is equally significant, because it centered on the personal relationships within Israel's society. This literary structure indicates that Israel's covenant relationship with God contained a vertical and horizontal dimension to it. Israel's love for God had to be demonstrated visibly in the way the Israelites cared for others. In fact, this idea was so fundamental to Jewish thought that when Jesus was questioned by a Pharisee hundreds of years later what the greatest commandment was, Jesus responded accordingly: "'You shall love the Lord your God with all your heart, and with all your soul, and with all your mind.' This is the greatest and first commandment. And a second is like it: *'You shall love your neighbor as yourself.' On these two commandments hang all the law and the prophets*" (Matt. 22:37-40, emphasis added). Jesus noted that the essence of authentic or true religion (which stood at the heart of the Law and Prophets) grew out of the two basic principles upon which the Decalogue was grounded.

The concern for others was primarily conceived in and tied to God's mercy and grace toward Israel. When the Israelites suffered oppression in Egypt, the text notes that God "observed the misery of my [God's] people who are in Egypt; I have heard their cry on account of their taskmasters. Indeed, I know their sufferings, and I have come down to deliver them from the Egyptians, and to bring them up out of that land" (Exod. 3:7).

God not only saw the Israelites' sufferings and heard their cries for help but also liberated them from bondage through his instrument Moses (v. 10). Just as the Israelites were recipients of God's mercy and care in a time of distress, so they were required to extend love and compassion toward those who were in need of assistance.

The Decalogue also functions as a prelude to the larger law code known as the Covenant Code in Exodus 20:18—23:19. Form-critical scholars have noted that this literary arrangement is intentional since all of the detailed laws that follow are really an outgrowth of the two principles upon which the Decalogue rests. Thus, the laws or instructions in the Covenant Code are like "case laws" or "living examples" of what it meant for the Israelites to love God and to love others. These laws were designed to promote order and stability in Israel's society so that the Israelites could flourish within their community and actualize God's blessing.

Many of the laws in the Covenant Code are geared toward living in relationship with others; laws, for example, that consider how one's actions affect individuals, either positively or negatively, in community, and others that focus on issues like generosity, justice, and compassion. The concern for the poor and vulnerable, in particular, undergirds many laws in the

Covenant Code. Within these laws, much attention is given to individuals such as the resident alien, the widow, and the orphan. Exodus 22:21-24, for example, states, "You shall not wrong or oppress a resident alien, for you were aliens in the land of Egypt. You shall not abuse any widow or orphan. If you do abuse them, when they cry out to me, I will surely heed their cry; my wrath will burn, and I will kill you with the sword, and your wives shall become widows and your children orphans."

This law addresses three main classes of people that were particularly vulnerable in Israel's society: the sojourner, who was landless and not a full-fledged member of the community; the widow, who did not have a husband to provide for her economic needs; and the orphan, who lacked basic parental and family support. Each one of these individuals was particularly susceptible to exploitation and abuse in ancient times. As a result, they were at the mercy of the larger community, and their economic and social well-being was dependent upon the kindness, generosity, and compassion of the Israelite people. Any violation of this injunction was serious, as God promised to pour out his wrath on the community if any of these people were mistreated.

The security and well-being of the alien, widow, and orphan is also apparent in Israel's agricultural laws and practices. More specifically, the law of the sabbatical year was designed to provide basic sustenance to the poor in the community. According to this statute, the Israelites were to farm their land for six years but were required to let it lie fallow in the seventh year. Not only did this agricultural practice give the land a rest (a Sabbath so to speak), but it also provided the poor in the community the opportunity to gather food to eat. The sabbatical law was broadened so that it applied to the harvest of olive orchards and vineyards as well (Exod. 23:10-11).

In terms of economic policy, the Covenant Code contains regulations concerning loans made to those who were facing economic difficulties. If there were Israelites who experienced financial hardships, they could secure a loan from other members of the community to meet their basic needs. This legislation (22:25-27), however, included an important caveat. The text notes in v. 25, "If you lend money to my people, to the poor among you, you shall not deal with them as a creditor; you shall not exact interest from them."

The law prohibited any Israelite from profiting from the misfortune of others. The lender was forbidden to take any interest on the loan that could place a greater financial burden on the borrower.

The same law also includes special regulations about accepting collateral on a loan. In biblical times, the borrower would provide his cloak as a guarantee that the loan would be repaid. However, the law stipulated that "if you take your neighbor's cloak in pawn, you shall restore it before the sun goes down; for it may be your neighbor's only clothing to use as cover; in what else shall that person sleep?" (vv. 26-27).

Some in Israel's society were so poor that the garment they gave in pledge was the only thing they owned to keep them warm at night. This provision ensured that the poor would not have to go without basic necessities while they paid the loan back. Violation of this law was especially troublesome in the days of Amos, and the prophet vigorously confronted individuals that failed to return garments at night (Amos 2:8).

Laws regarding the treatment of the vulnerable in Israel's midst are especially prevalent in the book of Deuteronomy. Whereas the laws of the Covenant Code applied to an agricultural society, the law code in Deuteronomy 12—26 presupposes a more settled, urban-like environment. City life tended to heighten the social ills that often plague a community. It is not surprising, therefore, that a number of the laws in Exodus were revised in light of this new historical and social setting. As a result, scholars have noted that Deuteronomy is more liberal in its call for the treatment of the poor and contains a more humanitarian strain to it.

Evidence of this is found in Deuteronomy's revision of the Sabbath law in Exodus. According to the Decalogue (Exod. 20:8-11), the Israelites were prohibited from working on the Sabbath, because God had sanctified it and established it as a day of worship. In Deuteronomy, however, the Sabbath law was revised to read, "But the seventh day is a sabbath to the Lord your God; you shall not do any work—you, or your son or daughter, or your male or female slave, or your ox or your donkey, or any of your livestock, or the resident alien in your town, *so that your male and female slave may rest as well as you*" (5:14, emphasis added). According to this legislation, the Sabbath was designed to give people (and animals) a day of rest from their labors. This revision was motivated by humanitarian concerns over the health and well-being of humans. Jesus appears to have understood the spirit of this law when he mentioned to the Pharisees that "the Sabbath was made for man" (Mark 2:27, NIV).

Deuteronomy's concern for the poor is particularly evident in the modification of the law regarding the release of slaves in Exodus 21:2-6.[2] According to Exodus, only the male was allowed to leave after six years of service. If he married during that time, his wife was not allowed to go with him. The woman could be redeemed by family, but only if her master was not pleased with her. The master could also designate her as a wife for his son if he so desired. In Exodus, the woman was essentially powerless and left to the mercy of her master.

Deuteronomy, however, allowed female slaves to be released from their service when eligible. Deuteronomy 15:12 states, "If a member of your community, whether a Hebrew man or Hebrew woman, is sold to you and works for you six years, *in the seventh year you shall set that person free*" (emphasis added). This law demonstrates Deuteronomy's kindness toward women in that it provided for their freedom and bestowed upon them the same legal rights as men.

The slave law in Deuteronomy contained a couple of other important nuances, especially as it related to the treatment of the slaves upon release from their master. In Deuteronomy, the slave was not to go out empty-handed. According to Deuteronomy 15:14, the master upon release of the slave was required to "provide liberally out of your flock, your threshing floor, and your wine press, thus giving to him some of the bounty with which the Lord your God has blessed you." This law ensured that the former slave would not go into society without basic necessities. This course of action reduced the likelihood that the freed person would become destitute and have to resort to becoming a debt slave again. Also, Deuteronomy allowed slaves to escape from their master because of abuse. In this situation, they were not required to return to their master if they had been mistreated before. They had the option to reside with the one to whom they fled, and they were not to be oppressed in any manner (23:15-16).

Deuteronomy also emphasized generosity toward one's neighbor; especially those who were poor. Deuteronomy contains laws regarding making loans to those in need. Like Exodus, the lender was not allowed to charge interest on the loan; whether the loan was in the form of money, provisions, or any other material item (Deut. 23:19). Like Exodus, the lender was to give the pledge of the poor person back before sunset, as this might be the only garment they had to wrap up in at night (Deut. 24:10-13). Deuteronomy, however, expanded this law by prohibiting one from taking a widow's garment in pledge (v. 17), since widows were at a distinct economic disadvantage. Deuteronomy also nuanced the law in Exodus in another important way. In Deuteronomy, the lender was not allowed to go inside someone else's home when taking the pledge (vv. 10-11). This proviso ensured that a measure of dignity and respect would be afforded to the borrower.

The call for generosity is also apparent in the instructions about the sabbatical year and the remission of debts. The law in Deuteronomy 15:7-10 states,

> If there is among you anyone in need, a member of your community in any of your towns within the land that the Lord your God is giving you, do not be hard-hearted or tight-fisted toward your needy neighbor. You should rather open your hand, willingly lending enough to meet the need, whatever it may be. Be careful that you do not entertain a mean thought, thinking, "The seventh year, the year of remission is near," and therefore view your needy neighbor with hostility and give nothing . . . Give liberally and be ungrudging when you do so, for on this account the Lord your God will bless you in all your work and in all that you undertake.

This law is particularly striking because it called upon the Israelites to give with a pure motive. According to this legislation, if anyone had an outstanding loan going into the seventh year, it was to be forgiven so that the borrower would not be saddled by the debt any longer. Such a law could, however, dissuade people from lending money, fearing that they would incur a financial loss. Incredibly, Deuteronomy exhorts its audience not to be "hard-hearted or tight-fisted," even if the year of remission was drawing near. Instead, the law encouraged the people to give liberally to the poor even if the lender took a financial hit. The author of this law reminds the people that God would reward them in their work and in all their undertakings if they gave with the proper attitude and spirit.

Deuteronomy also contained a number of other laws pertaining to the poor and needy of the community. It stipulates that the wages of the poor laborers were to be paid for before sunset (24:15). The poor could not afford to wait for payment, because they needed the money to provide for their daily needs. Deuteronomy also legislated that landowners leave those sheaves in the field that were dropped or left behind for the orphan and the widows to glean. Landowners were also instructed to leave some of the olives on the trees and grapes on the vine for people to harvest (vv. 19-21).

Deuteronomy, lastly, demonstrates a great concern for the Levite. Many times Levites are mentioned along with the widow, the orphan, and the sojourner as those who needed special attention and care. The reason for this is Deuteronomy 12:13-27 called for a central sanctuary where the Israelites would worship (most likely the temple in Jerusalem). As a result, the religious sanctuaries located throughout the country were closed down. This meant that the Levites, who served and ministered at these religious sites, were suddenly out of a job. The Levites, like the widow and the orphan, found themselves among the poor in Israel's society. This law ensured that the Levites would not be overlooked as the community would take care of the needs of those who provided religious guidance and instruction.

In closing, having compassion on those who were less fortunate was an integral component of God's covenant with Israel. The Torah provides many examples of how the Israelites could ease the suffering of the disadvantaged by exercising generosity and kindness in a myriad of circumstances. For the Israelites to be "a kingdom of priests and a holy nation" (Exod. 19:6, NIV), they were required to care for others in their community. The same mission exists for the people of God today, as the church is called to reach out in love toward those who are socially and economically at risk in our own communities.

• • • • • • • • • • • • •

KEVIN MELLISH is professor of biblical literature at Olivet Nazarene University. His area of specialty is Hebrew Bible. He and his wife, Jeanine, have long been active in ministries such as Smile Train (which provides surgery to children born with cleft lips) and child sponsorship through Nazarene Compassionate Ministries.

five

COMPASSIONATE MINISTRY AND EARLY CHRISTIANITY

Mark A. Frisius

One of the main contentions of this book is that the compassionate life should not be separated from holiness in the Christian life. Rather, they are integrated together and are the working out of faith in Christ. Compassion is not delayed in the pursuit of holiness but is part of becoming like Christ. The goal of this chapter is to test this thesis against the life of the early church. To accomplish this goal the manner in which early Christian authors connected the concept of holiness with compassion for others will be investigated in the light of the responsibilities of the Christian community and of the individual.

Why Consider the Witness of Early Christianity?

Over the last fifteen to twenty years, interest in early Christianity has distinctly grown, particularly within some evangelical circles. It is often seen as an attempt to return to a more pristine or pure version of Christianity that isn't yet tainted by modern philosophical systems. In particular, many evangelicals see early Christianity as being devoid of the trappings of modernism and the rationalism that accompanies it, which makes early Christianity ideal for communicating in a postmodern world.[1] In this way, early Christianity allows the modern Christian to engage with the gospel message from a very different set of philosophical presuppositions and moves the current reader closer to the original context of Scripture.[2]

This increase in interest has led to two common misnomers about early Christianity and compassion. The first is that Christian compassion and social concern only arose in the mid-twentieth century in response to Marxism and other elements of socialism.[3] Thus Christian compassion is simply seen as reactionary and having little to do with Scripture or the history of the church. The second is that modern Christians have rediscovered the biblical mandate for compassion, which was taught by Jesus but eliminated by Paul and the early church and replaced with legalism and doctrinal rigidity.[4] Thus, modern Christian compassion is a restorationist movement to remove (or at least get past) theological structures and simply return to being compassionate people.[5]

Compassion and the Christian Life

The main body of this investigation will be broken into two chronological sections. The first section will deal with the status of the church prior to the reign of Emperor Constantine (AD 306-37), while the second will deal with post-Constantinian Christianity and the changes that occurred with the legitimization and favoring of the church by Constantine.[6] The focus in both sections will be on the following elements: treatment of widows, orphans, and the poor; and how the life of compassion was connected with the life of holiness.[7]

Prior to Constantine

Overall, the witness of the early church fathers is that a life of holiness and a life of compassion are indistinguishable. That is, that one who is living an upright and moral life is engaged in compassion for others. This is such an extensive point that it is fair to say that their concept of the Christian life is not just about interior, personal transformation but also about what is done for others. In this, they often describe the moral and ethical fiber of the Christian in the same context as they do compassion for the poor, widows, and orphans. A key example of this is the *Didache*, which was an early second-century manual for Christian leaders. In chapter 4, the text joins the topic of giving to those in need with that of living in obedience to God's commandments.[8] It concludes that these elements are the way of life.

The majority of compassionate ministry in the early church was carried out by the bishops or the presbyters,[9] with the distinctive support of the laity. One of the main reasons for this practice is found in the demographic makeup of the early church. By and large, most people in the early church were poor and could give very little. The church would thus collect (usually following the Eucharist) a freewill tithe to support the charity of the church. Justin Martyr, a mid-second-century apologist, described the Christian worship service. He indicated that following the exhortation to do good things in imitation of the apostles, a collection was taken to care for orphans, widows, and strangers.[10] Soon after, Tertullian (d. AD 220) also described the worship of Christians, noting that it joins together the following of God's precepts with the support of the poor.[11] Thus, in early Christian worship, the movement toward a holy life was coupled with support for the poor and was seen as living a Christian life.

The bishop functioned as the administrator of the common fund and particularly kept track of the widows in the community.[12] Although women in the first few centuries AD had increased freedom, their rights and legal standing were still fairly limited and most were dependent on a male guardian.[13] When the husband died, poor widows were often left without the protection of a male guardian, particularly one who had legal standing to protect her interests. Poor widows would also lack a dowry, which would make finding a second husband difficult but not impossible. Lack of a husband or guardian would often lead to prostitution or begging. Early Christianity found this unacceptable and sought to meet the financial needs of widows in the cities. Beyond the biblical commands to care for widows, there were two main reasons for doing this: there was a distinctive value placed on the voluntary single life; and widows were able to make a unique contribution to the life of the church, particularly in educating the young.[14]

At other times, these funds were used to purchase the freedom of slaves or to otherwise redeem those who had been captured in battles. This work was seen as being too expensive to be accomplished by an individual, especially one who had very little means, and instead needed to be completed by the community under the auspices of the bishop. It is important to note that this commitment to the widow or slave would have been lifelong.

The early fathers are quite clear that this communal involvement does not absolve the individual Christian of his or her responsibility. Those who were able saw compassion as a requirement. Thus on an individual level Christians would help the poor or take in orphans. The type of aid that most Christians could offer to the poor was, by its very nature, limited and temporary; however, they were still encouraged and commanded to give. Many early Christian writers put together the imperatives to share with the poor and to follow God's moral commands, indicating the inseparable nature of compassion and holiness.[15]

The individual commitment to the orphan represented something within the realm of possibility even for the poorer families. The status of unwanted children in the Roman Empire was sad. Typically, an unwanted baby would be carried full term and born. Abortion was not usually considered, since it posed serious health dangers and denied a father his rights.[16] Therefore, most unwanted babies would be exposed, often in a place that encouraged other adults to find them. When exposure took place, three things could happen: death, slavery, or adoption.[17]

Christians would become known for searching the streets and the marketplaces for orphans in order to save them from certain death or slavery.[18] Adoption would represent a financial demand upon the family, because it was considered a lifelong commitment. However, the child would grow up to be a contributing member of the household as well, which is what enabled many of the poor families to proceed with adoption.

One of the most important elements of Roman society was a family name. This name provided identity and legal standing within society. In adoption, Christians would give an identity to a child who otherwise would lack identity and self-knowledge.[19] Early Christians understood that they were adopted by God, took his name, were made sons and daughters, and therefore should do the same for others. As Christ came to save them from slavery and death, so ought they to go out and save others.[20]

Overall, the testimony of the pre-Constantinian church suggests that there is a distinct connection between compassion and the holy life. Our compassionate actions toward others are inseparable from our moral transformation. These together are seen as complementary aspects of the Christian life. A second element is a connection with the Eucharist. In their conception, as we participate in our communal identity with Christ, we are drawn, corporately and individually, toward compassion for others.

Post-Constantine

When Constantine became sole Roman emperor in AD 324, he clearly favored Christianity and thus changed the trajectory of church and empire, including the compassionate outreach of the church. Constantine's presence enticed many wealthy and powerful people into the church, allowing for increased access to wealth and organization. However, many refused to give personally to the poor, believing their tithes and gifts to the church were sufficient and that the church alone should care for the poor.

The church leaders challenged this mind-set in a number of ways. First, they encouraged individuals to give to the poor before making extravagant gifts to the church.[21] Second, they challenged the assumption that the wealth of the church absolved them of the necessity to give. This was done by connecting the idea of compassion and holiness to form a composite picture of the Christian life.[22] In doing this, the church expounded on two intertwined ideas. The first idea was that there is nothing intrinsically good or evil about wealth or poverty, but what matters is how it is used.[23] The second element was encouragement to treat the poor with a sense of equality owing to the shared status of being created in the image of God. This allowed them to suggest that not only does Christ identify with the poor, but the individual Christian does as well.

Conclusion

One of the concepts that becomes clear from the church fathers is that holiness cannot be conceived of apart from compassion. They are intricately tied together so that the development of one goes hand in hand with the development of the other. Together, holiness and compassion compose the Christian life.

A second element is that the fathers very much developed a theology of compassion. Their understanding that each person was created in the image of God meant that followers of Christ had an obligation to address the social conditions of their contemporaries; that is, they could not idly stand by and watch the suffering of those around them. This obligation was met by addressing the practical concerns of the poor, widows, and orphans.

However, the church went further and began to establish a social doctrine. This meant not only meeting the temporary needs of the oppressed but advocating for change as well. These changes focused on advocating for justice for the oppressed, critiquing exploitation by those who ruled, and proposing concrete actions for change. In particular, these changes were related to the concept of the image of God, wherein human beings were seen as essentially equal regardless of their social standing.[24]

However, there were limitations to these proposals because certain injustices were seen as a natural consequence of the fall, which meant that certain social structures were seen as necessary and something to be endured. On these elements, the early church understood that it was not called to reform these unjust social structures but rather to improve the lot of the oppressed.[25] This is, perhaps, one of the areas where we could critique the early church, particularly as it applied to slavery, which was seen as a necessary part of life that could not be abolished. They could not conceive of a world without slavery partly because it was a result of the fall but also because it was simply the way things were.[26] Although it is possible to be overly critical of the church for lacking the realization that something could be done about unjust social structures, such criticism can lead the modern church to a helpful place of self-reflection, which is where this article will end.

1. What injustices in society do we simply accept as the way things are? What might be done to end the social ills that caused them? What can be done in the meantime to advocate for the rights and treatment of the oppressed? How as an individual can I meet the needs of the oppressed? How can the church meet these needs?

2. How can we continue to affirm the basic equality of all humans?

3. How might we preach social compassion and holiness as necessary parts of the Christian life?

4. How can we understand material goods as necessary for meeting the basic needs of humans?

5. How might we understand the giving of our goods as both a duty and an acknowledgment of the deep conviction that others are also created in the image of God?

• • • • • • • • • • • • • •

MARK A. FRISIUS is an associate professor of theology at Olivet Nazarene University. His area of specialization is the early church (patristics). He and his wife, Ellen, have adopted two boys from Korea.

six

CHRISTIAN HOLINESS TO SOCIAL GOSPEL
The Paradigm Shift of Person and Practice

Houston Thompson

• •

My wife and I were having breakfast one morning at a local restaurant. Our server was a young lady about nineteen to twenty years old whom we see occasionally and with whom we have developed a friendly relationship. From time to time she has shared her interests, perspective on her future, and hobbies. On this occasion, she was telling us about how she had just returned to community college to work on a general education diploma.

As the conversation continued, she proceeded to tell us that her mom's boyfriend moved out and that since she was in college and working, her mom invited her to move back and live with her. It was the next part of the conversation that surprised us. The young server said that she could live with her mom but only until she was about thirty years old. My wife asked, "Why thirty years old?" The young woman said, "I figure I will be tired of it by then, and I will be single and have a baby."

My wife continued to explore this by asking why she would be single; what about a husband? The young woman replied that she would have split up with her husband by then and be divorced. My wife asked if she didn't think she would find true love. The girl implied she wouldn't and then turned the questioning to us. She asked how long we had been married, to which my wife replied, "It will be thirty-eight years in August." My wife added, "And we still love each other." The server was amazed and commented, "That is not normal these days."

Just then she had to leave to serve other tables. As my wife and I talked, an elderly woman at a nearby table was leaving. As she did, she engaged the people behind her at yet another table. They were discussing the food, and the woman talked about how she learned to cook. She said, "I remember Daddy bringing home dynamite boxes from the mine and I would stand on them to cook." She said, "I've been cooking for over sixty-one years." Then she said, "Well, longer than that, I have been married for sixty-one years."

It was at that moment my wife and I looked at each other and had the same thought going through our minds, namely, how generational perspectives change. For the traditionalist at the other table, sixty-one years was just the norm. As boomers, and through the eyes of the server, we were atypical because we were still married. Our server, a millennial, just accepted as fact that by the age of thirty she would be married, divorced, and have a baby to care for as a single mother.

The perceptions of individuals change with every genera-tion. Today's generation may understand important values dif-ferent from their grandparents and possibly their parents. This makes it critical for us to understand values in the context of changes over time. This is true for our understanding of com-passion—especially as it relates to the Christian life. Current perceptions and practices of compassion reflect the influences of long historical development. We join a dynamic conversation with a formative historical context. Awareness of that context and the influences that have brought us here can help us consider our way forward as we think about the place of compassion in the life of holiness.

On the Road to Modernity

Across the historical development of Western society, the mores of society, the building of community, and even the establishment of laws were increasingly a reflection of the spiritual values found in the Scriptures and the classic Christian faith. A Christian worldview came to guide the thinking and actions of Christians and non-Christians alike in every aspect of life. The influence of this worldview profoundly shaped the understanding and practice of social outreach, or ministries of compassion. The work of compassion was the experience of a Christian worldview embedded in the life of Christian society.

For Christians this paradigm was nothing less than a biblical mandate. The transformational way in which a person experienced God and the demonstrative way a person conducted himself or herself provided the evidence of this experience. For the early church, it was most significantly manifested through the interactions the Christians had with others and the way in which they viewed community. The members of the early church displayed their holiness by living it out with those they encountered. One way the early church demonstrated their faith was by serving the needy through compassionate giving. Acts 2:45 states, "They sold property and possessions to give to anyone who had need." In chapter 4 of the book of Acts, Luke describes how the Christians shared everything they owned.

Economic compassion was simply an aspect of the life of the Christian community.

The church was known for her acts of mercy and social ministry. Christians literally cared for widows, orphans, the poor, prisoners, and others who suffered distress and misfortune. It was part of the culture of the church and remained a part of the culture for centuries. Social ministry was a natural expression of faith. These assumptions continued to shape Christian—and social—life in the West through the Middle Ages. Social welfare, care for the poor and marginalized in society, was the responsibility—and work—of the church.

Modernity

The Renaissance and the Protestant Reformation radically transformed early modern Europe. Among the many changes that resulted, responsibility for ministries of compassion began to be redefined. Civil legislative bodies began adopting some forms of social outreach as laws. Confiscated church properties, or their proceeds, were directed to serve the needy. In some cases, levies were placed on those in the community and the collections were distributed to parishes to be given to the poor. For those who could not care for themselves, financial assistance was provided. For those who needed residential care, facilities were established to provide that care. While the act of social outreach had government mandates, it was still closely linked to the church and a Christian worldview.

The Christian worldview long served as the backdrop for social outreach and introduced a new paradigm during the seventeenth and eighteenth centuries. The world was experiencing transitions resulting from the Enlightenment. The Enlightenment heightened our awareness of reason and accented the power of the intellect over experience. This period challenged the prevailing Christian worldview, shifting the conversation from faith and grace to scientific knowledge. Scientific discovery, based on the authority of reason, challenged the paradigm—and the authority—of a Christian worldview.

On the heels of the Enlightenment, industrialism was transforming society. The era known as the industrial age was introducing a new economy. Wealth as a value became more prominent. People were becoming self-reliant, with increased opportunities for earnings and amassing wealth. Social status became more fluid. The greater a person's economic worth, the more social status he or she had. The paradigm was shifting to more self-reliance, personal opportunity, and personal responsibility for one's own well-being.

The gap between those who were more financially self-reliant and those who were struggling economically broadened, leading to more disparity between the rich and the poor. Attitudes also changed as the self-reliant believed that good choices and hard work were the answer to self-sufficiency. In part, this led to the "Protestant work ethic" that saw economic prosperity as direct evidence of one's Christian experience. This sociological, and to some degree theological, shift redefined social expressions of compassion. The emerging attitude was that those who want to help themselves can help themselves, if they have initiative and work hard.

These sociological shifts were establishing a new norm; a new paradigm by which humans viewed the world and their responsibility in it in a new way. This modern worldview was empowering people to redefine, reshape, and refocus their lives. An increased reliance upon economics meant a person did not (or should not) need to rely on God or the community to meet his or her needs. This new paradigm did not embrace caring for others in the same way as the classic Christian worldview that predominated in the premodern period.

The Emergence of the Holiness Movement

In the latter part of the nineteenth century and into the twentieth century, the Holiness Movement emerged, particularly in the United States, drawing heavily from the Wesleyan/Methodist tradition that gave it birth. Early in our holiness heritage, holiness was taught and believed as a definitive work of grace. It began in salvation as a person confessed his or her sin and was justified, regenerated, and adopted into the family of God. Subsequent to conversion, there was a second experience known as entire sanctification, or the infilling of the Holy Spirit. It was this moment of entire sanctification when the sinful nature was transformed and the person was empowered to live the Christian life. At this moment an individual gave his or her life completely to God and relied totally on the grace, power, and providence of God.

This movement also connected the life and experience of holiness with ministries of compassion and the call to address social problems. It expanded the acts of mercy of the church to include social issues of the day. Churches and faith leaders engaged in outreach efforts in order to make a social difference. The expectation of radical personal transformation was connected to the expectation of societal transformation as the kingdom of God was manifested. During this time, there was an increase of orphanages, homes for unwed mothers, and similar social initiatives. Antislavery activism and advocacy for women were prominent venues of holiness in action. The Holiness Movement linked Christian values to social causes, demonstrating compassionate ministry as an expression of holy living. In this way it retained the historical link between Christian life and faith and ministries of compassion.

Modernity and Social Change

Modernism, ushered in by the influences of Enlightenment and industrialism, produced a decreased commitment and engagement with the lower socioeconomic and disadvantaged classes. Where Christians historically had helped those in need as expression of their spiritual transformation, reason and logic informed modernists to assume those who needed help could find it given the new economics of industrialism.

The events and movements of the twentieth century added to the sociological shift occurring and the paradigm people were increasingly embracing. Significant defining events—such as World War I, the Great Depression, and World War II—magnified the numbers of people suffering. In response, government programs, such as the New Deal, were introduced and began to do what the religious community had historically done. Compassion seemingly became the responsibility of civil government.

From a historic Christian worldview, outreach was something churches promoted as an expression and natural extension of the experience of faith. Giving sacrificially and serving others in need was simply part of the Christian's call and to a large degree took place through the church. Today, the paradigm has shifted. With the vast array of social programs in the Western culture (government, not-for-profit, and for-profit), churches became less engaged in social outreach. Perhaps, this has been by default as other governmental entities picked up the mantle. In any case, the primary responsibility for addressing social needs came to rest with the government and civil authorities.

Piety and Compassion

During the latter part of the twentieth century, Christians and churches started recognizing the crisis of need in the center cities, impoverished rural regions, as well as other areas, including those around the world. There was a renewed interest in outreach opportunities or compassionate ministry. However, the early church's view of helping those in need was still seen as relevant, but it had shifted from a core expression of faith to an activity as an example of faith. For some, compassionate outreach became an event that is planned, coordinated, and orchestrated periodically as another ministry event.

A dichotomy developed between scriptural holiness and social outreach. Holiness was now focused on a personal relationship with God in the context of community while outreach was focused on helping those in need, social reform, and justice. Holiness denounced a secular culture while outreach endeavored to change the culture. Holiness centered around the community of believers while outreach concentrated on the lost and disadvantaged.

Faith no longer encompassed all of a person's life, but became one aspect of the whole. A person's faith may or may not influence the other aspects of his or her life. Faith and other aspects of life can be mutually independent. Through these changing times, the Holiness Movement increasingly focused on an experiential relationship with God. It was not unusual to hear, "Jesus is the answer." This compartmentalization of faith led to a segregation of spiritual ministry and compassionate outreach. While the church valued helping those in need, the social problems and social issues of the day were nearly overwhelming. The challenge of liberalism created a perception calling for the church to preference either evangelism or the social gospel. Given that (false) dilemma, the evangelical church leaned toward evangelism.

Consequently, holiness and compassionate outreach became two separate issues. Holiness speaks to the personal relationship with God. Compassionate outreach is something a person may engage in as an avenue to make a meaningful difference and find personal reward. Social outreach, or compassion, became a choice separate from the experience of holiness. The two are not mutually exclusive. Many people of faith did—and do—engage in social compassion. But, while Christian faith and compassion may be linked, they are not necessary mutually dependent. Both theologically and practically, the problems of the poor and needy became increasingly distant from the life of the church.

Postmodernity

For the postmodern, faith may be defined by the social connections one makes. Engaging in an activity or event where one can give of oneself, do something tangible, or invest time and energy has become one way to define a faith experience. Many postmoderns would rather engage in a social outreach activity than participate in a structured corporate service or event. For some, compassionate outreach feels much more like the ministry of Jesus than participating in the traditional elements of a worship service.

The irony of this paradigm shift is the fact that, while compassion has become a prominent value among postmoderns, it was not nestled in a Christian worldview. The passion that drives social engagement had more to do with a sense of goodwill and helping others than a biblical mandate or expression of faith. For the postmodern, it is easy to separate the two. It is possible for an individual to engage in social outreach, even outreach built on Christian principle, without necessarily being Christian or connecting it to his or her personal Christian faith. This is also true for young people coming out of holiness churches. Formed to think of the issues of compassion and justice as, at most, an elective ministry of the church, they easily separate church and Christian faith from action in the world. The holiness church needs to capitalize on the passion of this generation to be meaningfully engaged and to make a difference. It is imperative that postmodern generations discover the breadth and depth of scriptural holiness and how it translates into authentic and altruistic service to others.

Recovering a Holiness Heritage

All of this has prompted efforts to reconsider the connection of scriptural holiness and compassion. There has been a resurgence of churches engaging in urban communities and other areas of socioeconomic need. Churches that left the urban areas decades ago are returning to the city with outreach ministries to effect change and touch the lives of those who are still there and struggling. In some cases, churches are starting compassionate outreach programs (e.g., food pantries, clothes closets, and counseling services) and trying to "get back to the basics." In a few cases, churches are starting not-for-profit organizations to structure and manage the compassionate outreach of the church. There is also an increased focus on global outreach leading to mission trips for the purpose of working and serving. Globalization has opened opportunities for churches to engage needs around the world. The church is reappropriating the work of compassion.

The challenge for the church today is to find an authentic narrative and expression of faith that grounds the understanding and practice of compassion in a Christian worldview. The key for the church is finding the compelling message that authenticates a faith grounded in a personal relationship with God while connecting to the needs of a secular culture. The message and actions of the church will have to be congruent and relevant to today's world. The church needs to be intentional about creating relevant conversations that point to authentic scriptural holiness as a personal and communal experience. The church should be reframing the calling of social ministry as the expression of communal holiness. The resources for this are readily available in our history, both in the deep Christian tradition and in our own Wesleyan-Holiness tradition. The church should embrace this ancient and traditional understanding of holiness that envisions the community of believers touching the world as a natural expression and practice of their Christian life.

Times change and our understanding and values develop over time. But we need not merely be passive inheritors of where history has brought us. The past represents legacy and resource. The future remains ours to shape.

· · · · · · · · · · · · · ·

HOUSTON THOMPSON **is the associate vice president for academic affairs and director of the Doctor of Education in Ethical Leadership Program at Olivet Nazarene University in Bourbonnais, Illinois. He is an ordained elder in the Church of the Nazarene and a licensed social worker in the state of Indiana. Prior to coming to Olivet, he served six years as the executive director of an interdenominational faith-based social service agency.**

seven

CONGREGATIONAL FORMATION FOR MINISTRIES OF COMPASSION

Phil Stout

• •

All of us believe in the ministry of compassion. Every Christian knows that we are called to feed the hungry, care for the poor, and stand up for the vulnerable. But too often there is a gap between what we believe and what we practice in local church ministry. There are a number of reasons for this. Some congregations don't know where to begin. Others are so overwhelmed with their own needs that they are convinced they don't have the resources—material or emotional—to confront the needs around them. Still others believe that ministries of compassion are the domain of denominational and parachurch ministries. They are supportive of those ministries but remain aloof from the needs in their own communities. But the greatest reason for the gap is that most local congregations have not been formed spiritually or theologically for Matthew 25 ministry—ministry to "the least of these" (v. 45).*

Here's a typical scenario. Within a local church there is a small group of people who are passionate about Matthew 25 ministry. Often they're given a designation such as the Compassionate Ministries Committee or the Benevolence Committee. They are convinced and committed. They try to launch local initiatives and raise the consciousness of the entire congregation. And the church is supportive of their efforts. But their efforts never become a broad-based ministry of the entire congregation. Because it is such a small percentage of the church that is given to this work, the projects are often seasonal and sporadic. While we would never allow ministries such as worship, prayer, evangelism, discipleship, and stewardship to happen a couple times a year, we seem to be all right with ministries of compassion being relegated to December or other onetime events. As hard as they try, this small cadre of activists never alters the direction of the church's efforts. Ministries of compassion remain a side issue in the work of the church.

Many pastors and church leaders yearn for change in this area. They long to see holistic ministry flourish in and through their local body of believers. But they realize that simply planning another event or sending a couple of people to partner with a local food pantry will not revolutionize a congregation for Matthew 25 ministry. That is because our major challenge is not structural or strategic. Structures and strategies for ministries of compassion can, and should, change with time, culture, and circumstances. The real challenge is theological and spiritual in nature. How can we be instrumental in forming—

---

*All Scripture quotations in this chapter are from the *New Revised Standard Version* (NRSV) of the Bible.

or even transforming—our congregations for the work of the whole gospel? How can our heads and our hearts change so that our hands and feet will follow? What movements must take place in our minds, spirits, and actions?

The Movement from "Either/Or" to "Both/And"

Let's be honest. For most American evangelicals, ministries of compassion are pretty far down on the list of priorities when it comes to local church ministry. Yes, almost every church has forays into this type of ministry. We send people on mission trips, raise offerings to dig wells, and partner from time to time with other agencies. But the prominence of Matthew 25 never comes close to that of Matthew 28—the Great Commission. After all, we've been taught that feeding a person is a temporary fix, while saving a soul has eternal consequences. So it has never felt like they should be anywhere close to each other in rank when it comes to the vision, priorities, or resources of a local church. For some, caring for the poor is like putting a small bandage on a gaping wound. It may seem like a nice thing to do, but ultimately it distracts us from the real work of the church.

Over the last century in America this manner of thinking has developed an "either/or" mentality. You either give yourself fully to saving the lost, or you give yourself to temporal solutions. You either give yourself to making disciples or you become sidetracked and lose your focus. This, along with old suspicions about the "social gospel," has left large swaths of the American church with the utterly preposterous concept that you must choose either the Great Commission or ministering to "the least of these." Imagine that. In essence what we are saying is that we can either take Matthew 28 seriously or take Matthew 25 seriously, but not both.

This has tremendous consequences. First of all, it enables a congregation to believe that ministries of compassion are optional. We can actually convince ourselves that we can be disciples without caring for the poor. The prophets and Jesus would disagree. James points us to an ill-clothed, hungry man and, if we neglect him, asks about our faith. "What good is it?" (James 2:14-16).

The church cannot afford an "either/or" mentality. It deprives us of genuine discipleship and the joy of being the body of Christ. It deprives God's children of the lives he has for them, and it makes it almost impossible for the world to see Jesus. Why did we ever think we had to choose?

The Movement from the "Future Only" Kingdom to the "Present/Future" Kingdom

Perhaps the major theological impedance to a full-orbed gospel is the dispensational theology that permeates American evangelicalism. With its firm belief that the "kingdom age" is yet to come, it de-emphasizes kingdom work in the present. The logical outcome of dispensationalism is an eschatology that teaches the annihilation of this planet rather than "the healing of the nations" (Rev. 22:2). The only goal for the true dispensationalist is preparation for the rapture and a world to come. It is no wonder that so many of them—even though they may have huge hearts for hurting people—see ministries of compassion as a distraction from the work of the gospel. As one prominent dispensationalist radio preacher used to say, "My job is to fish for men, not to clean up the fishbowl." Clever, but tragic.

It is of vital importance for a congregation to grasp the kingdom of heaven as a "present/future" kingdom, or as we sometimes like to say it, the "now/not yet" kingdom. Clearly,

Jesus taught these two aspects of the kingdom and we find great beauty in both.

It is hard to overestimate the debilitating effects of a belief in a future-only kingdom. Each year I ask my students to choose one of Jesus' parables that begins (as most of them do) with "The kingdom of heaven is like . . ." I then ask them to interpret the parable as if Jesus were speaking about a future kingdom only. Then I ask them to interpret it as if Jesus were teaching about the present *and* future kingdom. The difference is amazing. To reduce the kingdom of heaven to simply a future heavenly realm is to cut our congregations off from the true message of Jesus. A both/and kingdom theology opens our eyes to the richness of God's call on our lives in a dramatic and powerful way.

Opening our eyes to kingdom moments in the here and now is life-transforming. There is something sacramental about giving a bag of groceries to a hungry person. Breaking bread with a poor person is like breaking bread at the table of the Lord's Supper. God is present in a powerful way when a lonely child is embraced, the sick are attended to, and the prisoner is loved. When the homeless are invited into our churches, Jesus comes with them. We dare not deprive our people of these moments by allowing them to believe that the kingdom of heaven will come one day but is not a reality right now. The King has come and with him came the kingdom.

What we do for the future kingdom matters. What we do for the present kingdom matters. In fact, we really can't distinguish between the two. We Wesleyans are not dispensationalists. We labor and build for the here and now with the knowledge that the fullness of the kingdom still lies ahead.

You are not oiling the wheels of a machine that's about to roll over a cliff. You are not restoring a great painting that's shortly going to be thrown into the fire. You are not planting roses in a garden that's about to be dug up for a building site. You are—strange though it may seem, almost as hard to believe as the resurrection itself—accomplishing something that will become in due course part of God's new world. Every act of love, gratitude, and kindness; every work of art or music inspired by the love of God and delight in the beauty of his creation; every minute spent teaching a severely handicapped child to read or to walk; every act of care and nurture, of comfort and support, for one's fellow human beings and for that matter one's fellow nonhuman creatures; and of course every prayer, all Spirit-led teaching, every deed that spreads the gospel, builds up the church, embraces and embodies holiness rather than corruption, and makes the name of Jesus honored in the world—all of this will find its way, through the resurrecting power of God, into the new creation that God will one day make.[1]

Something wonderful happens when a congregation begins to internalize the present aspect of the kingdom of heaven. They begin to put their acts of compassion, mercy, and justice into a larger framework. They are able to connect the thing their heart tells them to do (which is actually the passion given to them by the Holy Spirit) to the plan that God has to redeem this fallen world. When they begin to make the connection, their hunger to serve grows deeper and stronger. Many will no longer be satisfied with typical in-house ministry. Committee meetings will bore and frustrate them. They will want people-on-people, life-on-life ministry because they have discovered Jesus in the hungry, the poor, the ill-clothed, the stranger, the sick, and the prisoner—just as Jesus said they would.

Part of the blessed task of church leaders is to help the body see that what God is doing in history is to be done through us—today.

The Movement from "Me" to "We"

Most of us spend our lives hanging our spiritual heads in shame when we read Matthew 25:31-46—the parable of the sheep and the goats. After all, who among us can say that we are fulfilling the task of feeding the hungry, clothing the naked, welcoming the stranger, and caring for the weak? We spend as little time as possible on that passage because it feels impossible. And, of course, it is. Impossible, that is, if we are viewing the gospel through an individualized lens. Yes, it is impossible for me. *I* can't do it. But *we* can do it. It is impossible for me, but it is not impossible for us. Forming a congregation for ministries of compassion necessitates moving them from the "me" of ministry to the "we" of ministry.[2] Hammering on Matthew 25 only induces debilitating guilt if it is heard as the mandate of the individual.

We know this to be true when it comes to evangelism and discipleship. We know that it takes a whole church to make one disciple. Gifts of hospitality, mercy, encouragement, evangelism, teaching, shepherding—and all of the spiritual gifts—are used by God in the making of every disciple. None of us were discipled by one person alone. We were (and are) discipled by the church.

The same is true with ministries of compassion. Just as I cannot and am not called to make disciples on my own (Matthew 28 ministry), so I cannot and am not called to accomplish ministry to "the least of these" on my own. When this becomes central to our thinking in the local church, it helps us make another movement.

The Movement from "Goat" to "Sheep"

Mark Allan Powell speaks about "empathy choices"[3] made by listeners throughout the course of a sermon. Literary critics use the word "empathy" for an "involuntary projection that causes us to identify with one or more of the characters in a story and experience the narrative in ways determined by that identification."[4] The meaning of the narrative and the impact of the narrative are determined by the involuntary empathy choice made by the listener. Powell illustrates empathy choice with the example of traditional western movies.

Hollywood turned out dozens of films celebrating the exploits of brave men who conquered the western frontier by triumphing over hostile savages. These films seemed to assume that their audiences would identify with the heroic cowboys and find the stories to be inspirational. Apparently, many people did experience them that way. Today, however, many viewers would be prone to regard such films as reflecting on a disgraceful aspect of American history. Why? Because they would empathize with the plight of the Native Americans in the stories and evaluate what is happening from *their* perspective. . . . Fans of these films did not consciously choose to identify with the cowboys as the "good guys" in these movies—they just did so with little awareness that anyone could ever experience the stories differently.[5]

Consider the impact of empathy choices in a sermon to an American congregation based on Jesus' parable of the sheep and the goats found in Matthew 25. It is easy to imagine a preacher identifying with the King ("clergy do seem to be more likely than laity to empathize with the character of Jesus"[6]) and easy to see middle-class Christians identifying with the goats. (Powell maintains that "if laity are offered a number of empathy choices, they tend not to take the idealistic route when a realistic one presents itself."[7]) The result would be guilt and quite possibly (even probably) de-motivating guilt because of the immensity of the problem of poverty in our world and the helplessness most Americans feel in the face of that issue.

Now consider a different approach, but not simply the approach that a pastor can take in one sermon. Rather, an approach to the atmosphere and tone of the church over time. Consider a pastor who helps the congregation make an intentional empathy choice in Matthew 25. The pastor helps the people see the hope of becoming one of the sheep who can show hope to a hurting world. The leader steps down from identification with the King and identifies as one who desires to be a sheep. In these empathy choices we go from the de-motivating guilt of "Depart from me, you who are cursed" to the hope of hearing the King refer to us as "you who are blessed by my Father" (Matt. 25:41, 34). It is important to keep in mind that empathy choices are usually unintentional. But a leader can explicitly promote an empathy choice for the congregation. He or she can purposefully invite people individually and collectively to see the narrative from a different vantage point. "Most people can switch gears when prompted to do so."[8]

When we, as a congregation, are participating together in ministries of compassion, we are collectively fulfilling the "well done" of the King. As the church attempts to embody the sheep of Matthew 25, everyone who is serving, praying, giving, and using their gifts to strengthen the church in any way are living as sheep. Even if their ministry is not seen as a "front lines" position in a particular compassionate ministry, they are still a body part in a body that is embracing "the least of these."

Of course, this then leads us to the importance of structure and strategy. We're not talking about empty words or simply putting a positive spin on the parable. We're talking about church leaders finding and creating opportunities for their people to have real, vital ministry to the vulnerable. We're talking about church boards who are allocating resources for ministries of compassion. We're talking about children's workers and youth workers who are giving our children real opportunities to serve the disadvantaged. We're talking about a commitment by church leadership to no longer feel guilt over Matthew 25 because they are leading their people to fulfill the mandate of Matthew 25.

One of the great moments in a church is when a pastor can report a victory in serving the disadvantaged. It is then that he or she can stand before a congregation and say, "Look at what God did through you!" (This is true of local ministries of compassion and of our partnership with denominational compassionate ministries.) God uses us—his sheep.

When we can humbly rejoice in being the face of Jesus to our community and to our world, Matthew 25 becomes one of our favorite parables.

The Movement from Angry Prophet to Pastoral Partner

When the prophets denounced the nation of Israel for their treatment of the poor and when Jesus revealed the hypocrisy of the religious leaders who "devour widows' houses" (Luke 20:47), their words were powerful and angry. And rightly so. They were uncovering sin of the most offensive nature in the eyes of God. But most of us in church leadership are not dealing with that (though it is certainly present in the governments and corporations of our world). What we are usually dealing with are people who do not realize the centrality of our obligation to the poor and who don't know where to start in fulfilling the call of Matthew 25. So our angry, prophetic words should be reserved for the structural injustices that permeate our country and the principalities that perpetuate those injustices. But our responsibility to Christ's church is of a different nature.

In his book *The Prophetic Imagination*, Walter Brueggemann leads us from simple prophetic proclamation to what he calls "prophetic ministry"[9]:

> I have tried to say that prophetic ministry does not consist of spectacular acts of social crusading or of abrasive measures of indignation. Rather, prophetic ministry consists of offering an alternative perception of reality and in letting people see their own history in the light of God's freedom and will for justice.[10]

Together we can live in a new reality—the reality of the present and coming kingdom. Together we can fulfill both the Great Commission and the call to care for "the least of these." Together we can be the face of Jesus Christ to our communities and our world. And we, pastors and church leaders, have the privilege of forming congregations into these alternative communities that are the answer to the prayer Jesus taught us to pray—"Your kingdom come, your will be done, on earth as it is in heaven" (Matt. 6:10).

•••••••••••••

PHIL STOUT **is senior pastor of the Jackson, Michigan, First Church of the Nazarene. This dynamic congregation has grown to over fifteen hundred, with a special focus on community and compassionate ministry.**

eight

THE CALL TO COMPASSION

J. K. Warrick

• •

Today, we have about eleven hundred compassionate ministry centers around the country. On the one hand, we celebrate that evidence of the expanded practice of compassion in our churches. On the other hand, we really should have over twenty-nine thousand compassionate ministry centers, because every church should be a center of compassionate ministry and evangelism. In every community where there's a Nazarene church, there ought to be the heart of compassion, because you cannot separate the call to holy living from the call to get involved in the world in which we live.

I want to give some biblical context. I want to work from Luke 10, the parable of the good Samaritan, talk just a little about that parable, and then share some of my own journey in this whole topic of compassion, evangelism, and ministry.

On one occasion an expert in the law stood up to test Jesus. "Teacher," he asked, "what must I do to inherit eternal life?"

"What is written in the law?" he replied. "How do you read it?"

He answered, "'Love the Lord your God with all your heart and with all your soul and with all your strength and with all your mind'; and, 'Love your neighbor as yourself.'"

"You have answered correctly," Jesus replied. "Do this and you will live."

But he wanted to justify himself, so he asked Jesus, "And who is my neighbor?"

In reply Jesus said: "A man was going down from Jerusalem to Jericho, when he was attacked by robbers. They stripped him of his clothes, beat him, and went away, leaving him half-dead. A priest happened to be going down the same road, and when he saw the man, he passed by on the other side. So too, a Levite, when he came to the place and saw him, passed by on the other side. But a Samaritan [and this would have been a terrible insult to this Jewish teacher], as he traveled, came where the man was; and when he saw him, he took pity on him. He went to him and bandaged his wounds, pouring on oil and wine. Then he put the man on his own donkey, brought him to an inn and took care of him. The next day he took out two denarii and gave them to the innkeeper. 'Look after him,' he said, 'and when I return, I'll reimburse you for any extra expense you may have.'

"Which of these three do you think was a neighbor to the man who fell into the hands of robbers?"

The expert in the law replied, "The one who had mercy on him."

Jesus told him, "Go and do likewise." (Vv. 25-37)

The parable of the good Samaritan is a parable we read often. It speaks directly to us about our involvement in the world. It's a reminder that Jesus called us to be in the world but not of the world, to be aware of our culture and aware of our surroundings. There is much of the culture where we can involve ourselves, and we should. Let's involve ourselves and be representative of kingdom values in whatever is happening in our community. That's the call of God, *in* but not totally *of*, participating but not capitulating, giving ourselves to the task of connecting but not giving ourselves away to the flow of cultural influence—and that's God's call to all of us, to be in this world but not of the world.

I fear sometimes that in the Church of the Nazarene, with our emphasis—and it's a good emphasis—to live lives that are somewhat separated, we may have drawn the lines too deeply in too many places, and we might need to erase some of those lines. Maybe we've distanced ourselves too much in some areas and rendered ourselves almost irrelevant to the great needs of the world in which we live, and God is calling us to a place of relevance. The gospel is always relevant. What we do demonstrates the relevance of the gospel. In this parable we find a man who saw a need and moved to meet that need. There was no church surrounding him. There was no one there to encourage him. But you get the idea that this may have been a lifestyle with him.

In this parable there were others who passed by and probably felt some sense of responsibility and obligation. Generally when people feel that, if they're not going to respond to it, they move to a distance. How easy it is just to play as if the needs aren't there or to think that the needs belong to somebody else. Someone else is responsible for this, but I'm not responsible. If we can just look away, it will go away, or at least we'll be absolved of responsibility and we can go on about our business. The priest and the Levite were probably doing good things, and on their way to important tasks and responsibilities, but they missed an opportunity to do something that was so very much like God.

When Jesus came, according to Luke, he claimed this Old Testament truth that he would proclaim the gospel and give sight to the blind, that he would bring healing to those in need of healing, that he would proclaim liberty to those who needed release, and that he would proclaim the favor of God. And not only proclaim it, but he would live it out in his personal life so that everyone everywhere would come to understand that Christ had come into the world for them. If they would open their lives to him, he would move to meet immediate needs, even as he moved to meet everlasting and eternal needs, and that's the call of God.

I was very interested in an article in *Christianity Today* in March of 2013. It was an article titled "Here Come the Radicals!" It's a story of a group of young pastors around the country whose favorite word is "really." "If you're really a Christian," "if you're really committed, then you will really do this, and you will do it really often." "Really" is their big word, and it expressed their commitment to actually ("really") living out the Christian life. But the last paragraph of this particular article was, I thought, very insightful. It's a good insight and it struck me.

For us in the pews, testing ourselves must include deliberating about our vocations and whether we are called to missions, or to a life of dedicated service to the poor, or to creating reminders with art and culture of the gospel's transcendent, everlasting hope. Discovering a radical faith may mean revisiting the ways in which faith can take shape in the mundane, *sans* intensifiers. [That is, without the special emphases. When does faith take hold without the special programs or the special trips or the special opportunities?] It almost certainly means embracing the providence of God in our witness to the world. The Good Samaritan wasn't a good neighbor because he moved to a poor part of town or put a pile of trash in his living room. He came across the helpless victim "as he traveled." We begin to fulfill the command not when we do something radical, extreme, over the top, not when we're really spiritual or really committed or really faithful, but when in the daily ebb and flow of life, in our corporate jobs, in our middle-class neighborhoods, on our trips to Yellowstone and Disney World—and yes, even short-term mission trips—we stop to help those whom we meet in everyday life, reaching out in quiet, practical, and loving ways.[1]

In other words, compassion is a lifestyle. It is not something that we do; it's who we are. If the heart of a holy God has filled us with his holy love, then it's not simply to love him, but it is to allow him to love a broken world through us. That means that we live lives that are interrupted occasionally. We find ministry opportunities at the most inconvenient times, and yet we respond to those opportunities because this is our priority. Church meetings, church programs, church plants, and all the machinery of the church that is important to us is not ultimately our priority. Our priority is to do what Jesus would do if he were here, and that's what God calls us to do.

So Jesus had to go to Samaria, and Jesus had to pass by that little tree where Zacchaeus was perched, and he had to go by the blind, and he had to stop and take care of the lepers, and he had to stop and take care of the woman with the issue of blood. All of those were interruptions in his life. They weren't on his agenda. They certainly weren't on the agenda of the disciples, but it was a way of life for him. God calls us, even those of us in ministry, to live this kind of life. This is the call of God. In the *Christianity Today* article they talk about a new Holiness Movement. Isn't it interesting that they would identify compassionate ministries with a Holiness Movement, because it is so much like God himself.

The Lord called me to preach when I was a young man. I answered that call to preach, and I only have one ambition in my life, and it's still the only ambition I have with regard to ministry. I want to be a holiness preacher. But more than I want to be a holiness preacher, I want to live the life of holiness in a way that makes sense. I want my life to demonstrate what I say.

I was involved in reaching out to poor people in my first church. I used to get up on Sundays and go out and pick children up. I remember sitting in a home with the rats running across the floor. It was just not a good place to be. But I felt that if Jesus were here, he'd be going to these people. He'd care about them. Patty and I got lots of food in that little church. People in the congregation would bring stuff and actually give it to you, just because they liked you and loved you. We gave much of that food away to people in need. It was just something we felt we should do. Later, in subsequent church assignments, we made similar efforts. But God wanted to take our efforts at compassion to another level.

We were in Cincinnati. Patty had a bus route; I had a bus route. I would drive the bus on Sunday morning and pick kids up and get them into Sunday school and preaching, and then take them home Sunday afternoon. It just seemed like the right thing to do. Sometimes Patty would go in and get them dressed in the mornings, and it was reaching out to people who were suffering and hurting. But I really didn't think about that in terms of a holistic ministry.

Then we got involved in the Lamb's in New York City. That was a real shock to my system. Paul Moore, the founding pastor, was there, and I was really captivated by their ministry. They just were simple, sometimes uncouth, people but something special was happening. If somebody got shot on the street, they'd drag him into the lobby of the church. Whatever happened in the church on Sunday seemed to have some immediate impact on the streets, and that captured me. Most of the people in Cincinnati didn't even know that the church I pastored in Springdale was meeting. There was no immediate impact from what happened to us on Sunday and what happened in the streets, and there was no immediate impact on us from what happened in the streets. We would read about things in the newspaper and hear about hunger and pray about it, but there was no impact. But here in New York what happened was so immediate and impactful, both inside the church and outside the church.

Over time we went on several Work and Witness trips that returned and worked at the Lamb's Club. When Paul Moore resigned, I got a call appointing me as pastor of the Lamb's Church. That was a call that shook my world. I was born in Oklahoma, raised in South Texas, and pastored in Ohio. We're not New York, New York, kind of people, but we were intrigued. So we went and we met the board. We prayed about it, and I kind of wanted to go, but Patty wasn't sure. "This is way beyond us. It's not us. It's out of . . . it's just not us." We continued to pray about it, and finally she said, "If that's what you think we ought to do, I believe I can do that. I'll do that."

At the same time I was in prayer and fasting with our Sunday school superintendent on a Friday. We met, and I was praying about the Lamb's. As we were praying and fasting, God spoke to me that day, and he said, "Johnny, you can't go to the Lamb's, and I will never allow you to pastor a church in the heart of the city, but I will hold you responsible for the well-being of the cities where you serve. I'll hold you responsible." And that was a life-changing moment for me.

We eventually moved to Indianapolis, and Dean Cowles came and joined our staff. We were going to have a Thanksgiving feast for our people, and I said in a meeting one day, "Well, before we do that, we need to have a Thanksgiving feast for people in the inner city." And Dean, like Isaiah in chapter 6, said, "Let me do it, let me do it!" So Dean took that on and began to put it together. We had that meal, and before long, two or three couples from Westside were moving into the heart of the near east side of Indianapolis, and what we now know as Shepherd Community was born. Our church family began to pour time and energy and involvement and money—lots of money—into that mission, and it was a healing thing for our church family. It brought renewal to us. It brought unity to us that we deeply needed. Something better happened to us than ever happened in the city. God just began to move in a wonderful way.

We started another church in Center on the west side of town, in an effort to reach the part of the city that Indianapolis had fled. You know, we have to stop running. Somehow we've got to be willing to embrace our communities and put our arms around them and love them. It's what Jesus did. He moved into our neighborhood, not out of our neighborhood. He didn't run from the darkness in our lives. He didn't run from the sin in our lives. He didn't run from the brokenness. He ran to us and took all of that to himself, and we as the body of Christ must run to them, and take the hurt and take the pain and take the shame and take the brokenness. Take it to ourselves and bear that for them so that they can see the love of God and know that the heart of God is for them. He's for them. He's not against them. He's not angry at them. God is angry about sin, but he's not angry at people. He loves people, and we have the opportunity to demonstrate that. God isn't running away, and we need to stop running too.

Over the final years of my pastoral ministry, we continued to find ways in Indianapolis and Olathe. We never could get into the downtown of Kansas City. We tried so many different ways for four or five years. It seemed as though all the doors were closed, and we discovered needs and brokenness in the community of Olathe, and we were able to purchase a six-plex from some builders in the church, and we opened a home, a healing place for mothers, single mothers with children. We worked with Mid-America Nazarene University. They offered tuition reductions and elimination for some of these young mothers, and we offered free childcare in our learning center. They got their GEDs, and some of them got associate degrees. Not all of our efforts were successful, but some took hold and somebody got it. A life was changed, children were delivered from the cycle of generational poverty, and their lives were forever changed.

In Indianapolis, at Shepherd Community a few years ago they had their first graduate from Olivet. And they're having graduates now from other colleges and universities, young men and women who have been caught up in the love of Jesus. They discovered that somebody loved them, and they realized that life can be better than they thought it could be. They don't have to live entrapped in the brokenness and dysfunction of a lost world. There is an answer, and the answer is Jesus, and we showed them the way, and we demonstrate that by emptying ourselves in order to reach them.

I just never got over that Friday, and I'm not over it today. I'll never get over that, when God broke my heart for people whose lives are challenged and broken, and the call that he put in my heart not to have special programs and special emphases, but to live a life that engages broken people with the good news and the powerful love of the Lord Jesus Christ. I believe that's God's call to every preacher, to every layperson, to every church, particularly every Church of the Nazarene. We are holiness people, and when we are constrained by the love of God we can't look another way. We can't turn our eyes. We look at the needs, and we move into the need with redemptive love, because our God can change the lives of broken people.

I was recently at Westside for a service, and I looked in the choir and saw a young lady. I remembered the first time she came to Westside. Her mother wanted to put them in school. I believe that if you have a Christian school you have to make a way for anyone to go. If you're going to have a private school, then you can keep people out because they don't have money. If you're going to have a Christian school, then you have to make a way for anyone to come. This mother had four children, and she wanted her kids to come to our school. She didn't have any money, so we made an arrangement with her. She could help in cleaning the building when she could work it into her schedule, and that would pay the tuition for her children.

So, they came to Westside and they were accepted and they were loved. They would have had difficulty in the public schools because of their cultural makeup and their racial makeup. They would have had difficulty, but one of those kids was elected president of the student body of the Westside Christian School. She's singing in the choir at Westside, teaching a Sunday school class, and is a schoolteacher today because a church said, "We will be Jesus to you. We will love you; we will make a way for you. God will make a way."

The Lord has saved all four of those children. One of those young boys is in ministry now, and that's just because of people who are saying, "We're going to do this in Jesus' name." That's the good Samaritan. Just living like Christ and in the course of our lives we touch the broken and the disenfranchised. No matter how inconvenient, no matter how great an interruption it is, we do it in Jesus' name. My prayer for all of our churches is that we will all be a compassionate ministry site, every church a house of compassion. A church should not only be a house of prayer but also be a house of compassion, where people of all walks of life, with all manner of needs, will know that here's a place where they can come for help.

We were in a prayer meeting at College Church one night of the week. We had every night of the week someone praying, and one night a lady walked in off the streets, and didn't know anybody there, and she asked one of our employees who happened to be out in the lobby. She said, "Is this the church that prays for people?" And they said, "Yes, it is, and they're praying now." And she came in and saw the ladies gathered around her, and they began to pray with her, and she was wonderfully converted, and they began to disciple her and she began to come to church, and her life was a mess and a challenge for us, but not a challenge for God, and God in his infinite grace began to work in her life. Every church should be a center of holy compassion. If we meet their needs, we earn the right to tell them about the great Healer, and that's what God calls us to do and that's who he calls us to be. Thanks be to God.

I want to invite you to hear God's call to compassion together with me. This is not an invitation to be saved or sanctified. But it may be a call to a new way of living. If you listen, God may be talking to you about how your life should be spent or how your church should be defined or shaped. If we will listen, he will call us where we need to go. If we will allow him to place his heart in us, to live his heart through us, we cannot fail to find compassion in the heart of holiness.

• • • • • • • • • • • • •

J. K. WARRICK **is a general superintendent of the Church of the Nazarene, noted holiness preacher, and an advocate for holiness compassion.**

CONCLUSION
AT THE HEART OF HOLINESS
Carl M. Leth

• •

What is the place of compassion in the holy life? We have explored the answer to that question in Scripture, the deep history of the Christian church, in our own tradition's history, in our theology, and in our practice. By now the answer should be clear. Compassion is at the heart of holiness.

This includes understanding the heart of holiness as a moving center of our feelings. Seeing brokenness and need, the heart of holiness is moved as the heart of Jesus was moved. Holiness produces a tender, responsive heart that sees the hurt around us as our concern. It is our concern because it is God's concern. We should be moved because he is moved.

But compassion goes beyond feelings of empathy or concern. It is a disposition of life, the expression of a fundamental character of living as a Christian. It is a way of living that translates God's heart of compassion into caring and redemptive action. When we actualize compassion we reflect the life of the One who came to us in the history of redemption, from the activity of the God of Israel to the ultimate action of love in history, the incarnation. Loving us, he "emptied himself" (Phil. 2:7, NRSV) even "while we were still sinners" (Rom. 5:8). He acts.

We have remembered that this way of living has been characteristic of Christians and Christian communities from the earliest era of the church. And we have been reminded that this way of living has been embedded in our history as a tradition. It has been the "holiness" way. This is no new proposal for a creative redirection of our tradition. Rather it envisions the recovery and practice of the life of the Holiness Movement in its most vibrant expressions. It represents "coming home" to our tradition at its best.

At the same time we have seen that this is not only faithfulness to a vibrant past but also an opportunity for a vibrant future. This is an engaged, holistic vision of Christian life. It offers a way of understanding compassionate activity in the world that is connected to a richer vision of what God is doing—and will do—in the world. It brings the various expressions of brokenness and pain in the world into the view of God's redemptive work. These are all venues of action and healing for holy, redemptive love. Further, the bold optimism of the Wesleyan-Holiness tradition enables us to act with expectation and imminent hope.

For societies and generations disillusioned by religious communities who seem disengaged from the brokenness and need of our world, this vision of Christian life offers an engaging way forward. Christianity—holiness—as a way of living in the world is combined with an optimism of hope and expectation of transformation for persons and communities.

We can abandon the limiting assumptions that pose compassion and authentic evangelism as contraries. In fact, evangelism can only be authentic when conjoined to an expectation and practice of transformed living. That transformed living involves both the journey inward and the journey outward. The energies and dynamic of the two together create a powerful synergy of kingdom life.

There are, of course, other issues and challenges facing the church in these rapidly changing times. This conversation about the place of compassion in the life of holiness is only part of the broader conversation. This issue does not answer all of the questions facing us. But we have seen that—whatever else involves the life of holiness—at its center we must certainly find compassion. It is the heart of holiness.

FINDING OUR WAY FORWARD

Jay Height
Director of Compassionate Ministries,
USA/Canada Region, Church of the Nazarene

• •

We call ourselves Christ followers. We strive to follow in his footsteps. We want to be holy as he is holy. So, as we think about compassion, we need to follow in his footsteps again.

In John's Gospel we find a beautiful portrait of the compassion of our Christ. John the Beloved helps us see a glimpse of how Christ demonstrated compassion.

In John 4 we see Christ engage in a conversation with the woman at the well. First, we see Christ going to a place where Jews did not go. Samaria was the community of half-breeds. Other Jews making the same journey from Jerusalem to Judea would typically follow a path that led them around Samaria, not through it. That added many miles to the trip, yet no "good Jew" would go to Samaria.

But the compassion of Christ would not limit where he would go and who he would engage. Christ's compassion would not be limited by political correctness or cultural taboos of the day. So why was Jesus in Samaria, a forbidden place? It

FINDING OUR WAY FORWARD

says he had to go there. What would make him go to a place like Samaria? The answer is clear. The only reason he had to go was because his Father sent him.

In this encounter we see him living out his compassion. He begins a conversation with a woman who, by the reputation and character of her life, was a woman that no respectable Jew would be speaking to. The fact that she was at the well during the middle of the day is the result of her rejection by her own community because of her lifestyle.

How did Christ express his compassion? He confronted her in her sin. You're living with a guy who isn't your husband and you've been married five times, he says? Try that opening line at your local coffee shop? Compassion? It doesn't sound like it. Yet, I contend it was pure compassion. He knew that if he didn't address this reality in her life, she would always wonder, "If he knew me, would he still care for me this way?" Sometimes compassion needs to confront sin.

In the next chapter of John we see another compassionate encounter. Jesus asked a paralyzed man, "Do you want to get better?" That's an interesting question to ask—unnecessary, even provocative. But in over twenty years of urban ministry I have learned that you cannot help someone who doesn't want to be helped. After Jesus healed him and sent him on his way, John tells us that Jesus sought him out (probably after a few days) and said, "Stop sinning or something worse will happen." Jesus models compassion in both healing and conversation.

These two chapters give us a profile of the compassion of Christ . . . a combination of both the cross and the cup of cold water.

The compassion of Christ is the natural expression of his holiness, and so it should be for us. The message of this book is that compassion and holiness belong together. This means that our holiness churches should also be centers of compassion. Every holiness church should be a center of compassion. Every ministry of compassion should be an expression of the character and life of holiness—and should include a call to holiness. As we move forward, this is the vision of compassion—and holiness—that should capture us.

Allow the Father to sanctify your heart and help you live out a life of compassion. For a broken and suffering world may our lives reflect the Christ we follow until it is true that "they will know we are Christians by our love."

Reflection Questions

1. All his compassionate work did two things: it gave glory to the Father and created relationships with humanity. Is your compassion doing that?
2. Is your compassion fueled by your holiness?
3. Do you care as much about the cross as you do the cup of cold water? Do you care about the temporal and the eternal?
4. Is your compassion a lifestyle, not a to-do list?
5. Are you going to broken people, are you seeking them out?
6. Is the Father compelling you to go to the neglected quarters of our cities and communities, and are you obeying?
7. Can you define the theology and how that understanding shapes your expression of God's holiness through your life?

• • • • • • • • • • • • •

JAY HEIGHT is the executive director of Shepherd Community Center, a leading compassionate ministry center in Indianapolis, and serves as Nazarene Compassionate Ministries coordinator for the USA/Canada Region of the Church of the Nazarene.

NOTES
•••

Chapter 1

1. Mildred Bangs Wynkoop, *A Theology of Love: The Dynamic of Wesleyanism* (Kansas City: Beacon Hill Press of Kansas City, 1972).

2. Thomas Merton, *Conjectures of a Guilty Bystander* (New York: Image Books, 1968).

3. Elizabeth O'Connor, *Call to Commitment: The Story of the Church of the Saviour, Washington, D.C.* (New York: Harper & Row, 1963).

4. Gordon Cosby passed away on March 20, 2013, at age ninety-five, spending his final days in Christ House, a hospice for homeless people organized by the Church of the Saviour.

5. Elizabeth O'Connor, *Journey Inward, Journey Outward* (New York: Harper & Row, 1968).

6. In December 1975 the Community of Hope Church of the Nazarene began meeting at the Potter's House in Washington, D.C. In 1980 I became the founder and director of the Community of Hope, Inc., developing a comprehensive neighborhood organization to address a wide variety of inner-city problems. The Community of Hope (communityofhopedc.org)—now with an annual budget of $15 million with over two hundred employees—has developed several programs including housing for homeless families, health care, legal aid, job training, and educational, recreational, and social programs for children and youth. These programs now employ more than forty staff with a budget of $1.5 million. The distinctive emphasis of these programs has been to develop comprehensive, coordinated services to address the spiritual as well as the temporal needs of economically disadvantaged people in the inner city of Washington, D.C. The Community of Hope has been cited in the national media and in awards for its innovative programs to address the problems of inner-city neighborhoods. The Community of Hope Church of the Nazarene continues its ministry in a new location in southeast Washington, D.C., near the new Community of Hope, Inc., center.

7. Thomas G. Nees, "The Holiness Social Ethic and Nazarene Urban Ministry," DMin thesis, Wesley Theological Seminary, March 1976.

8. Molly Worthen, *Apostles of Reason: The Crisis of Authority in American Evangelicalism* (New York: Oxford University Press, 2014).

9. Albert C. Outler, ed., *John Wesley* (New York: Oxford University Press, 1964).

10. See: http://usacanadaregion.org/sites/usacanadaregion.org/files/PDF /Books/John-Wesley-Christian-Revolutionary.pdf.

11. Donald Dayton, *Discovering an Evangelical Heritage* (New York: Harper & Row, 1976).

12. Timothy Smith, *Revivalism and Social Reform in Mid-19th-Century America* (Nashville: Abingdon Press, 1957).

13. Worthen, *Apostles of Reason*, 179.

14. David O. Moberg, *The Great Reversal: Evangelism Versus Social Concern* (New York: Lippincott, 1972).

15. Stan Ingersol, *Rescue the Perishing, Care for the Dying: Sources and Documents on Compassionate Ministries in the Nazarene Archives*, 2nd ed. (Kansas City: Nazarene Archives, n.d.).

16. David O. Moberg, *The Great Reversal: Evangelism and Social Concern*, rev. ed. (New York: Lippincott, 1977).

17. "Minutes of Several Conversations," Q.3, in *The Works of John Wesley*, vol. 8, edited by T. Jackson (Grand Rapids: Baker, 1978), 299. This gave Wesley's Methodists a distinctive identity. It also gave them a distinctive mission. See more at: http://www.catalystresources.org/consider-wesley-37 /#sthash.DnkxA8oU.dpuf.

18. Tom Nees, *Dirty Hands—Pure Hearts: Sermons and Conversations with Holiness Preachers* (Kansas City: Beacon Hill Press of Kansas City, 2006).

19. Mark Quanstrom, *A Century of Holiness Theology: The Doctrine of Entire Sanctification in the Church of the Nazarene: 1905 to 2004* (Kansas City: Beacon Hill Press of Kansas City, 2004).

20. C. Nathan Funk and Abdul Aziz Said, *Islam and Peacemaking in the Middle East* (Boulder, CO: Lynne Rienner Publishers, 2009).

21. Jonah Sachs, *Winning the Story Wars* (Boston: Harvard Business Review Press, 2012).

Chapter 4

1. Leviticus does contain legislation regarding the poor, especially as it relates to agricultural laws (19:9-10), paying wages (19:13), and instruction regarding the sojourner/alien (19:34). Due to space consideration, however, my attention will be devoted to the laws in Exodus and Deuteronomy where most of the legislation regarding the poor is found.

2. We should not think of slavery in the Old Testament as it occurred in American history. In ancient Israelite society, people became slaves in order to pay off a debt or a loan. It was not an institution that enslaved a group of people on the basis of their race or ethnic background. Biblical law allowed for debt slavery, although it was carefully regulated and limited to a period of time.

Chapter 5

1. Robert Webber, *Ancient-Future Faith: Rethinking Evangelicalism for a Post-modern World* (Grand Rapids: Baker Books, 1999), 28-29.

2. Christopher A. Hall, *Reading Scripture with the Church Fathers* (Downers Grove, IL: InterVarsity Press, 1998), 19-38.

3. Peter C. Phan, *Social Thought*, Message of the Fathers of the Church 20 (Wilmington, DE: Michael Glazier, 1984), 15-16.

4. This is a connection of two major themes within what has been termed the "emerging church." The first theme is a distinct emphasis on social justice, which is often placed before matters of theology (Rob Bell, *Velvet Elvis: Repainting the Christian Faith* [New York: HarperOne, 2005, 2012], 167). The second theme is a desire to return to the "authentic" teachings of Jesus, which were distorted by Paul (Scot McKnight, "The Ironic Faith," *Christianity Today* 52, no. 9 [Sept. 2008]: 62).

5. Often one or two historical people are identified as examples of compassionate Christians, leaving the impression that the rest of the church had missed the mark. Two of the more common examples are Francis of Assisi and Mother Teresa. One notable exception is Shane Claiborne, who acknowledges that there is a strong history of support for the poor within early Christianity (Shane Claiborne, *The Irresistible Revolution* [Grand Rapids: Zondervan, 2006], 327). However, what is often missed when citing the early church fathers is the tremendous weight they put upon right belief (orthodoxy) alongside right behavior (orthopraxy).

6. In AD 313, Constantine would sign, along with a co-emperor, Licinius, the Edict of Milan, which legalized Christianity. Against popular belief, Constantine never made Christianity the official religion of the Roman Empire, rather he gave Christianity preferential treatment.

7. Some notes will be made on the reaction to the slaves as well, although that topic will be saved for the conclusion.

8. The *Didache* is available at www.newadvent.org/fathers.

9. The separation of the bishop from presbyter appears to have occurred in the early second century. Prior, each local church was typically governed by a council of elders, with each elder referred to as both bishop and presbyter. It would be in the writings of Ignatius of Antioch that the emergence of a single bishop surrounded by a group of presbyters would start to ap-

pear (Hans Van Campenhausen, *Ecclesiastical Authority and Spiritual Power in the Church of the First Three Centuries*, translated by J. A. Baker [Stanford: Stanford University Press, 1969], 84-107; Francis A. Sullivan, *From Apostles to Bishops* [New York: Newman Press, 2001], 103-25).

10. Justin Martyr, *Apology I*, chap. 67. Available at www.newadvent.org /fathers. It is significant to note that the goal of any apology in the early church was to present a public explanation of Christianity. In nearly every apology, the explanation included a connection of Christian morality and compassion.

11. Tertullian, *Apology*, chap. 39. Available at www.newadvent.org /fathers.

12. Keeping the roll was one of the earliest responsibilities of the bishop. First Timothy 5:9 mentions the list of needy widows that was kept in Ephesus and presumably in other churches as well.

13. If a woman had three or more children, she would have the right to inherit part of her husband's estate. This was a great benefit to the wealthy widow, but poor widows had nothing to inherit. In the ancient Roman world, approximately 40 percent of the women between forty and fifty were widows, which equaled nearly 30 percent of the overall female population (Bruce W. Winter, *Roman Wives, Roman Widows: The Appearance of New Women and the Pauline Communities* [Grand Rapids: Eerdmans, 2003], 124-27).

14. Geoffrey D. Dunn, "Infected Sheep and Diseased Cattle, or the Pure and Holy Flock: Cyprian's Pastoral Care of Virgins," *Journal of Early Christian Studies* 11.1 (2003): 3.

15. Irenaeus, *Against Heresies* 4.13.3. Available at www.newadvent.org /fathers. Aristides, *The Apology of Aristides*, 15. Available at www.newadvent. org/fathers. *Didascalia Apostolorum* 4.3 (3.2). Available at www.earlychristian writings.com/text/didascalia.html.

16. Peter Garnsey, *The Roman Empire: Economy, Society, and Culture* (Los Angeles: University of California Press, 1987), 136-38.

17. W. V. Harris, "Child-Exposure in the Roman Empire," *The Journal of Roman Studies* 84 (1994): 1-3.

18. Typically, orphans would either be adopted or fostered (Cornelia B. Horn and John W. Martens, *"Let the Little Children Come to Me": Childhood and Children in Early Christianity* [Washington, D.C.: Catholic University of America Press, 2009], 163).

19. Adoption provided a change in legal status and name. In fact, many Roman adoptions were meant to provide a family with a suitable heir (Hugh Lindsay, *Adoption in the Roman World* [Cambridge: Cambridge University Press, 2009], 87-90).

20. Francis Lyall, "Roman Law in the Writings of Paul—Adoption," *Journal of Biblical Literature* 88 (1969): 466; Sarah Julien, "Coming Home: Adoption in Ephesians and Galatians," *Quodlibet* 5, no. 2-3 (2003).

21. John Chrysostom, *Homilies on Matthew* 45.3; 50. Available at www.newadvent.org/fathers.

22. John Chrysostom, *Homilies on 1 Corinthians* 21.3; 25.3. Available at www.newadvent.org/fathers. The success of the church in encouraging compassion can be seen in Emperor Julian's attempted restoration of paganism, in which he encouraged pagans to emulate the charitable activities of Christians (Julian the Apostate, *Epistle* 84a, in Robert M. Grant, *Early Christianity and Society* [San Francisco: Harper, 1977], 124-25).

23. John Chrysostom, *On Wealth and Poverty*, translated by Catharine Roth (Crestwood, NY: St. Vladimir's Seminary Press, 1981).

24. Phan, *Social Thought*, 28.

25. Ibid., 28-30.

26. Slavery functioned to save lives in the midst of warfare and served as a potential solution to a personal economic crisis. The church would also buy and either keep or release slaves when possible and always advocated for better treatment.

Chapter 7

1. N. T. Wright, *Surprised by Hope: Rethinking Heaven, the Resurrection, and the Mission of the Church*, repr. ed. (New York: HarperOne, 2008), 208.

2. The verbs describing the actions of the sheep in Matthew 25:35-36— *edokate* (you gave), *epotisate* (you gave drink), *sunegagete* (you entertained), *periebalete* (you clothed), *epeskepsasthe* (you visited), and *elthate* (you came)— are second person plural. While this is not conclusive to my assertion that the call is for the community, it is in harmony with it.

3. Mark Allan Powell, *What Do They Hear?: Bridging the Gap Between Pulpit and Pew* (Nashville: Abingdon Press, 2007), 29-31.

4. Ibid., 29.

5. Ibid., 30-31.

6. Ibid., 56.

7. Ibid., 57.

8. Ibid., 61.

9. Walter Brueggemann, *The Prophetic Imagination*, 2nd ed. (Minneapolis: Fortress Press, 2001), 116-17.

10. Ibid.

Chapter 8

1. Matthew Lee Anderson, "Here Come the Radicals!" *Christianity Today* 57, no. 2 (March 2013): 25.